A
JOURNAL
OF THE
FLOOD
YEAR

A JOURNAL OF THE FLOOD YEAR

A NOVEL BY

DAVID ELY

DONALD I. FINE, INC.
New York

Library of Congress Cataloging-in-Publication Data
Ely, David, 1927–
    A journal of the flood year / by David Ely. — 1st ed.
        p.   cm.
    ISBN 1-55611-272-6
    I. Title.
PS3555.L9J68   1992
813'.54—dc20   91–55172
                                                            CIP

Manufactured in the United States of America

10 9 8 7 6 5 4 3 2 1

Designed by Irving Perkins Associates

to Roberta Pryor

PART
ONE

JULY 12

I don't yet know what this is going to be—a report or a journal or just a few notes—but this is the beginning, and the beginning is the Wall.

I am worried about what is happening out there.

To get the basic fact down: last Tuesday, almost by chance, I discovered heavy salt concentration in the drainage trench running north from Km 44 to Km 56, where it begins tailing off.

This means that there is a twelve-kilometer saline front along this part of the Wall.

The stuff is ankle-deep, half muck and dead weeds; the rest is heavy brine.

The important thing is that the sensors have missed it. Not only have the sensors missed, the backups have missed. There is nothing on the tapes. The flashboard is blank.

When I signaled Dr. Matthews at Northeast, he said the sensor and backup systems were in perfect order. If they didn't show salinity, it was because the amount was negligible.

I told him that, in my opinion, based on personal verification, the amount was in excess of what could be called negligible, but

3

he said visual sightings were guesswork at best, and asked me about something else.

I just hope the Deeps have caught it.

JULY 13

I went out to the Wall and took brine measurements at a dozen places.

No matter how many times I visit the Wall, I always have the overwhelming sensation of its strength—and I am tremendously aware of the Atlantic booming out there, too. The fact that you can't see it from the inland side makes it all the more impressive. On stormy days it sends spray beating up; some drifts over the top.

The brine in the trench doesn't come from spray. There is too much for that.

It must be seepage. There is no other possible explanation.

And it must be of recent formation—within the past three weeks.

On my return to the Neptune office, I sent another red flash to Northeast—the third this week—and they replied with a 1203. Everything under control.

But the salinity is still there. More, if anything. And if things are under control, why don't the sensors and the backups register it?

JULY 15

Writing these notes is a strange experience for me. I hardly ever write anything. I can't remember the last time. For reports and other official records I use the voxit. That would be enough in this case, too.

Except I am quite troubled now about the Wall.

And I feel the need for this separate and independent record.

So I am using one of those late-model midget micropens. It is thumb-sized, with a storage capacity of something like a billion words. A new wrinkle is that you don't need to press it against anything when you write. It will write in air if need be. (Right now I am scribbling away on the palm of my hand, because it seems more natural that way.) Of course, "writing" isn't an exact term since the words are stored inside the pen. With this model you don't need any special attachment to read over what you've set down; you just snap the cover and it will project against whatever is in front of it.

Writing this way gives me an odd feeling, as if it's something private and personal that will draw things out of me I wouldn't ordinarily let go of. I have an impulse to write about Hilda, and Bloom, and my experiences with the stimulator.

I realize that none of these things belongs in an engineering report. If that's what this is going to turn out to be.

I am responsible for the entire Baltimore Canyon region, an office I have held for three years now, but I have never met Dr. Matthews or any of the other top staff people at Northeast headquarters in Boston. They haven't come down here, and I haven't gone up there.

Dr. Matthews is on the other end of my telemin, which is all I've ever needed for practical purposes—and I don't care about getting to know the man personally; I've met plenty of his type, and they're all pussyfooted little bureaucrats with hobbies like collecting antique bottle caps or baseball cards.

But when something like this comes along, I'd like to be able to look him in the eye when I explain to him just how serious I think the situation may be.

JULY 16

This past week I have become very damned uncomfortably reminded of the fact that we are living on an ocean plain—the Shelf.

It is a valley one million square kilometers in size.

We took it from the ocean—and the ocean wants it back.

That's why I worry when I see brine in the ditch.

Dr. Matthews can say that visual sightings aren't worth a damn—but he lives inland.

I can't put in for a transfer to a safer place. I'm on probation for three more years, which means I'm stuck here. I could retire, but something in me rebels at the idea of quitting so early in my career, especially now that there is seepage out at the Wall. This region is my responsibility, and I intend to find out what's going on.

Bloom refuses to believe that there is anything wrong with the sensors and backups, and he has begged off going out to the Wall to see for himself, arguing that he is a technical supervisor, not a field man. "You've done your duty, Commander," he says. "Let Northeast decide."

But Northeast has already decided—and they're wrong.

Hilda was feeling tired last night, and didn't want to get into the stimulator, so I decided to use the Telesex random scan, and picked out a promising set of tactile energy readings. Julia was the name on the scan slot. She was fresh and vigorous, and the experience was more exhilarating than is usual with randoms, but I couldn't help wondering if she wasn't really a stock model. Bloom used to work in the Telesex Center helping rig them up, and he swears you can't tell the difference. The idea of it, though— I don't know, it puts me off, and when you don't know for sure one way or the other, naturally that gets you thinking maybe it's one of the stock models.

Maybe that's what Julia thought about me. That I was a stock model.

If she wasn't one herself.

JULY 17

I am writing this sitting on top of the Wall, looking out over the Atlantic.

The ocean is slapping and chopping about thirty meters below—it's high tide—and every now and then it gives a real punch, sending up the spray. This page is speckled with salt.

When I was younger I used to climb the Wall like a monkey, working my way up from one chink or crevice to the next. Some climbers used pitons and ropes, but I never did. God knows why I wasn't killed. That was when the guided tours still came out, and I guess I wanted to show off for the people standing down there gawking.

I'm still a young man—only fifty-six—and in top shape, but I wouldn't risk a climb if there weren't this place where they left in the old rungs and spikes. You have to use gloves, though. Those spikes are rusty.

Climbing the Wall is like entering a different world. You get the feel of it in your blood: the cold rock, the smell of salt, the fear of falling. The Wall isn't just stone. There are patches of rockweed and vines, and colonies of crabs and ants and sandfleas in the crevices that mill around agitated and amazed to see you bellying over them. Now and then you'll come across a gull roost with that sulphurous gull-stink in it, or white sea-flowers scattered like tiny stars on the granite, and when you look up to see the sweep of Wall above you, you have the sensation of riding a vertical raft in the sky.

I used to walk the top of the Wall. Once I walked north all the way across the Canyon juncture up to where I could see the impact-energy intake structure at the Hudson Towers—but I never walked after I saw a couple of men killed just ahead of me on a stormy day. I'll never forget it. One got blown off into the ocean and the other went over the inland side, 150 meters down to the embankment ledge, and they wouldn't let us see him, they said his head was like a wet rag.

Something like a dozen walkers used to get killed every year.

Then they made climbing and walking illegal, and put in the patrols.

The top of the Wall where I'm sitting is covered with lichen and seagull shit. I can feel the Atlantic beating, I can actually feel it through all that rock . . . is that possible, or is it my imagination?

Now in the distance—looking south along the top of the Wall—I can see the patrol ursid coming my way. He must be at least a kilometer away, but he has picked up my silhouette; they are set to register anything bigger than a gull. He isn't moving fast—they build them slow-tracked so they won't get blown off, but even so they lose one now and then—and I've got about five more minutes before I have to start down.

God, it is beautiful up here. Looking north you can see the Wall running straight as the edge of a knife before it disappears in infinity. South—where the ursid is coming from—it begins bending inland where the Cape May depression starts.

Straight east is water, water, water—and the submerged humpback ridge of the breakwater. The ocean boils over it. It's white there, a foamy froth like hot cream.

Behind me—I mean west—there are the flatlands, ten kilometers across. Salt grass and beet fields mostly, and here and there an equipment shed and storage silo. The rest is pitch pine and scrub oak.

Rearing up at the far edge of the flatlands is the Rampart, grassy and wooded, with roads snaking up its side, and some houses visible. From here it looks like an ordinary range of hills, but with binoculars you can make out the shape of the pilings in places where the original facing has eroded.

That ursid is getting closer. They move on all fours to keep low against the wind, but the head stays fixed in the one position all the time, looking straight ahead. Gives me the creeps.

I came out at noon to measure the depth of the brine in the trench. It was about the same level as before. I couldn't tell any difference, except it sure wasn't lower, but it's absurd when you think of all the micro control systems planted inside and outside and all up and down the goddamned thing—as Bloom says, "Every time a clam sneezes, there's a wiggle on a screen somewhere"—and here is the regional engineering director in his rubber boots, wading around in the drainage trench, poking a steel tape down into the muck to see if the Wall has sprung a leak.

Yesterday I got Dr. Matthews on the telemin and laid it on the line about the salinity, asking him sarcastically if he wanted me to bring him a bucketful of the stuff to prove I was right—and he got very stiff with me and said he was relying on the evidence of infallible control systems, not human guesswork, and informed me that, as far as he was concerned, the subject was closed.

I called him back this morning, but he was in conference. So they said.

I'll start down in a minute. I hate to leave; wouldn't, if it weren't for the wind coming up, blowing spray, which could make it slippery.

Not to mention the ursid. He's getting closer. The weatherproofing stuff they dip them in gives them a weird, shaggy surface. His lenses are shiny, like wet plums.

They say they don't do anything except hold you and signal— but I heard of a case where a man was held for an hour before the patrol craft hovered up, and there wasn't much left of his arm by then.

I'm going down now.

JULY 18

I woke up this morning depressed; the pillowcase was damp with sweat, and my teeth ached from grinding—a sure sign of bad dreams.

I had the impulse to go in to Hilda's room, but I knew she would just tell me to take an EZ pill and get into the comforter for a few minutes . . . and I didn't want to do that. I don't know what I wanted, but I didn't want that.

I can't stop thinking about the Wall.

It isn't the salinity that troubles me so much as the sensation that Dr. Matthews and the rest of them up at Northeast not only don't know that the sensors and backups aren't functioning, they don't want to hear anything about it. As far as they are concerned, everything is checking out, no problems of any kind, and who is this madman down at Baltimore Canyon sending red flashes and yelling over the telemin?

Bloom surprised me yesterday. He is such a rabbit, never venturing a remark about anything controversial, but he spoke to me openly on this question, advising me to keep quiet, saying that I shouldn't risk annoying those people. "It's your word against the systems, Commander," he said. "You can't go against the systems."

"I know what I've seen. If they don't believe me, I'll find someone who will. I'll go over their heads if I have to."

"You can't do that, sir. It's against regulations. You'd face disciplinary action."

"I've been disciplined before."

Bloom hesitated, blinking his little eyes at me, and then he said, so deliberately it almost seemed as if he'd rehearsed it: "It might be worse this time, Commander. A lot worse."

That troubled me. I know what that "worse" would be—but they wouldn't dare try that, there would be no basis for it, as I am just doing my duty.

Still, the idea stuck in my mind. I haven't been able to get rid of it.

What was Bloom trying to do—frighten me?

And did he think of it himself?

I doubt it. He's too timid to have opened his mouth about such a thing on his own.

I can't help wondering whether Dr. Matthews told him to give me a warning.

Everybody is wearing American flag-pins today. It is Freedom Day, commemorating the Freedom Act of '31, known as the Second Bill of Rights, establishing the right of each citizen to enjoy a healthy and pain-free longevity, and the full development of his or her capacity for physical pleasure.

I'm wearing my pin, too, although I'm not given to displays of patriotism. This is one time, though, when the politicians are right. We have attained the highest possible point in world civilization, and the Freedom Act symbolizes this for all of us, regardless of sex or religion or genetic makeup, and the guarantees it embodies can never be taken away from you.

Provided you don't get excluded.

JULY 19

The Shelf has a rotten climate. No wonder so few people choose to live here. The ocean winds come in cold and salty all winter and halfway through the spring; the damp gets into your bones. In the summer doldrums, the air is thick and heavy, and you feel suffocated. No matter what they say about the effectiveness of the drainage and soil-building programs, on some days the whole Shelf Valley smells like dead fish.

I supervise thirty-seven subordinates, the only human one being Bloom—the rest are felids and murids—and Bloom gets on my nerves. He is skinny and freckled, and cruises around the control room in a powerchair, whistling between his teeth. He's a good technician, really a wizard with his hands, I have to admit—there's nothing he can't fix—but I get irritated by his whistling and his cracking his knuckles and his obsession with the Telesex stimulator, that's all he thinks about, he just can't leave it alone, and then he insists on calling me Commander—that being the Navy equivalent of my Interior Department rank—it's Commander Fowke this and Commander Fowke that all day long. He must know it annoys me. Maybe that's why he does it.

Whenever I try to talk to Bloom about the seepage problem, he backs off. He won't even listen. "Don't rock the boat," he says. "Think of your career."

I know what he means by that, but it is inconceivable that they would even consider such a drastic step to silence me. They couldn't get away with it. I may have bent the rules now and then, but I have broken no law.

Let them try.

There is one thing that would be worse than exclusion, anyway, and that would be getting underneath a few trillion megatons of green salt water.

JULY 20

The Wall was the single biggest construction project in the history of the world.

Its completion increased by one-tenth the land area of the continental United States, the equivalent of Montana and California combined.

The wave-impact program provides one-third of national energy requirements. Inland Valley food and mineral production has added at least twenty-five per cent to national totals.

Etc., etc.

This is a record we can be proud of.

Frankly, I wouldn't care if it didn't do anything but stand there.

As someone wrote once—who was it? I can't remember—beauty is its own excuse for being.

The Wall is beautiful.

Humankind is constantly developing and improving. There is no better proof of this than measuring the change in attitudes over the centuries, as I do on occasion by skimming through Librex references in ancient literature. I ran across something yesterday by Spinoza: "Man is a social animal." This may have had a certain truth to it back in primitive times of tribal huddling and interdependence, but it makes no sense at all today. We are self-sufficient now. We do not need others. Technical progress has enabled us to live without the physical closeness and group contact that led inevitably to rivalries, aggression, and war.

Man is *not* a social animal.

* * *

Saw a program on the Vidipix last night about the "mother" songs that were so popular back in the 19th and 20th centuries, a very funny show; in fact, Hilda got to laughing so hard the tears were running down her face.

The program quoted figures showing how close we are to eliminating viviparity. It is about 99.9 per cent, except among the excluded, of course, where they still do that.

For women, it must be quite a relief to be free of such a disgusting and humiliating ordeal. Hilda says she knew a mother once when she was a girl, a neighbor down the street, and she said it made such an impression on her, it was the most shocking and horrible spectacle she'd ever witnessed, the woman's stomach bloating up like a monstrous balloon, and then her screaming when the baby came out all bloody and howling, really a bestial thing, and it must have a terrible psychological effect on them. Just the thought of it makes me ill.

The Freedom of Genetic Information Act lets you find out the identities of your sperm and ovum suppliers—that is, their ribonucleic codes.

I once had my codes interpreted, and the analysis agreed with the placement series I took in high school.

I have a strong sense of responsibility and order, plus a good level of mathematical ability, which made me a natural for engineering administration, but there is also a chromosomatic wild card in my deck—"creative diametrics" is what they call it in the genetic catalog.

No one will admit it, but your chances for career advancement are pegged to your codes, which means I can't expect to rise higher than the third Civserv category.

They don't want troublemakers—and that's what "creative diametrics" amounts to, to judge from my own experience.

I have a short temper and don't take orders very well, unless I happen to agree with them.

If someone steps on my toes, I step on theirs—harder.

That's what happened in Memphis—I was chief field manager for the Mississippi–Gulf Interchange System—when they put me on probation and transferred me up here.

I doubt that people like me are used as genetic donors any more. This wasn't true back when I contributed, though, so I suppose I've passed along my diametrics to a few "sons" and "daughters."

I may even have some "grandchildren" by now.

My name, William G. Fowke, came out of the name-pool.

The G. doesn't stand for anything.

JULY 23

The 9:00 A.M. Neptune-Baltimore airbus is just lifting off.

We are still in the shadow of the Rampart, but the upper part of the slope is beginning to catch the sun. This accentuates the irregularities of the terrain—the defiles and glacises the topographic engineers worked into the design to make the Rampart seem natural, not like what it is: a second-line backup . . . just in case.

Now we are rising above the Rampart ridge-line; the Wall is coming into view behind it.

I am profoundly moved every time I see this sight. Up close, the Wall is overwhelming, it is like being under some giant skyscraper or some great dam, or a mountain cliff that shoots to the clouds; but from up here in the sky, looking down and seeing the pure horizontal sweep of it, it takes your breath away, for you are aware of its godlike, majestic scale.

For me, the Wall is a work of art, a masterpiece in steel and hydrofex and granite. You can go up in a satellite, it is true, and see it all—from Nova Scotia down to Fort Pierce, Florida—but you cannot grasp it completely even then, I mean the sheer grandeur of it cannot be fully comprehended by the mind of any single man, and so it is infinite, because it goes beyond the horizon of human experience in some way, and never comes to an end.

One passage in a speech President Leavit made last year has stuck in my mind, and it goes like this:

The Wall is our principal national monument, symbolizing as it does the finest and most enduring qualities of our great country. It stands as a testimonial to the courage and determination of the generations of Americans who devoted their talents and energies to building it—and it is a memorial to those who gave their lives during its construction.

Plenty of them died. The East Georgia cave-in, for example. That was the worst. A thousand killed. It must have been terrible. But that didn't stop us. Nothing stopped the building of the Wall.

These are the kinds of thoughts that go through my mind when I see the Wall—how much it cost us in lives and blood, and how much it has given us, not so much in material benefits as in . . . I don't know how to put it, exactly, but it is a spiritual thing, a historical thing. It is like a great battle which we won. It is splendid in itself.

That's why when I am sailing through the sky seeing the Wall back there below with the ocean brimming up behind it, and the sun beating down on the water, turning it the color of brass, and the clouds skimming in like great white birds, I can't help feeling a surge of pride and patriotism and just plain professional admiration.

I'm glad I don't fly this line very often. Inland Valley Transit Corporation puts its oldest equipment in this underpopulated zone—Neptune has about eight thousand people, and there isn't another town until you get to South Poseidon, fifty kilometers west, and that isn't much bigger than Neptune. This bus ought to have been retired years ago. It's got rust patches here and there, and the seams are loose—you can feel drafts blowing along the aisle—and the engines sound like sick lions howling. The felid-pilot who flies it has a spring sticking out of its back plate. That hardly inspires confidence.

Besides, the seats are too close together for my comfort. I am nearly two meters tall, and broad in the shoulders and the beam. I need space. After my last trip I was so disgusted I went to the airport office to register a complaint, and I must have gotten a bit worked up, diametrically, because I remember splitting the counter with the fist I was using to emphasize my remarks, and the manager threatened to call the police. I should have torn the place apart. IVTC is a monopoly run by bookkeepers and pissants who do nothing except suck the public's blood.

Looking back, I can't see the Wall any more. The Rampart is just a smudge on the horizon.

We are heading due west, and the whole Valley is spread out below.

It is in its way as remarkable a creation as the Wall itself—just think of the decades of effort required to drain and de-salt all this, what a stinking wasteland it must have been—but it doesn't give me the same lift I get from the Wall. It is like Ohio or Indiana down there: wide rolling fields of wheat and corn, and big patches of woods, with open pasture here and there—except you don't see any little towns, and there are few farmhouses, since most farms are operated by track-robots. People never have been attracted to the Valley, except down at Hatteras. Life is better in the West.

Partly it's fear. Nobody wants to admit it, but the idea of living on the Shelf—with that wild ocean out there slamming away day and night trying to get back in—

It worries me, too.

We are just south of the Cape May heights now. At this point you can see the shadow of the old shoreline running beneath the fields, a ghostly trace of that dead reach of ocean.

I registered this trip as day-off time. I didn't want to let Northeast know I was intending to see Dr. Grandgent, and I would have had to specify my destination if I had logged it as duty.

That I don't want to do. Under the Defense Secrets Act, we are forbidden to discuss internal questions with anyone on the outside. You can't go to the media, you can't even go to your congressman. They would have to report you; otherwise, they'd be in trouble. Even seeking the views of such a respected authority as Dr. Grandgent is taboo.

I will be in hot water if my visit to him is discovered—and if someone up at Northeast wants to make an issue of it.

I don't trust those people. They are capable of doing anything to justify their position—there is nothing more vicious than a nest of bureaucrats if you stir them up—and I will have to run a certain amount of risk to do what I think is right.

Which is to force them to see the truth, that something potentially very dangerous may be building up in the 44–56 Km sector.

Of course, the Deep systems should be sealing that area.

I say "should be" because I am not taking anything for granted now.

Up ahead I can see Chesapeake Bay. They still call it that, even though it isn't a bay but a valley. The central part—from the Kent Plateau down to the Patuxent Tunnel—is like a giant checkerboard, with dozens of ponds for shellfish cultivation. I can see some of the robotenders down there—they look like crayfish from this height—crossing and recrossing the ponds, feeding and pumping, and dragging their selector nets behind them to harvest the mature specimens.

Now Baltimore.

I've seen the big photogram mockup of the city as it was in 2048 before the port was closed and the bay mouth blocked. It was quite prosperous-looking, even though the move west was well under way by then (the capital had just been moved to Denver).

Baltimore is a different place now.

In the city center there are maybe thirty buildings still standing:

office blocks and apartment towers. Some are in use as warehouses. The rest are empty, except for the birds and rats. There are trees growing out of them.

In the old days the city administration knocked down most abandoned buildings and used the rubble for harbor fill. They intended to create parks and gardens in the cleared areas, and planted grass and flowering shrubs, but with the tax base so reduced, they couldn't afford the cost of maintenance, and had to let everything grow wild. What you see—we're at a hundred meters now, and the balloons are out—is a sort of jungle down there, with privet and rose and wisteria and honeysuckle jammed and choked and tangled up together, a green sea surging around these few desolate buildings with their windows bricked up or boarded shut.

Only around the Lombard–Pratt terminal and the shellfish packing plants in the Monument–Park zone is there regular commercial activity.

The main avenues are kept clear; the rest are all pitted and overgrown.

The people that work here live in the suburbs and commute by airbus. There aren't many of them.

Dr. Grandgent has a house up beyond the old Johns Hopkins site and won't move out, even though I and other ex-students of his have been after him for years to leave.

He is one of the few viviparous persons I know—and is not at all embarrassed by the fact. He even keeps a photograph of his parents on top of the piano. I try not to look at it when I visit him. If I had a skeleton like that in my closet, I wouldn't keep it on display. But then, he is of a different generation.

The backup felid has just opened the doors. Everybody out.

I am out on North Maryland Avenue beyond the canneries, watching for the murid.

It must have begun tracking me at the terminal, when I rented the single-wheeler. Of course there are so many of them around—messengers, carriers, sweepers, etc.—that you don't think twice about them, and I was out near the old U.S. 40 viaduct before I realized that the little devil was tracking me at a thirty-meter range.

Just to be certain, I circled the next block—no easy trick, with the side streets smashed up and overrun with weeds—and it stayed right on my beam: whenever it came to a stretch blocked by wild privet, the damned thing just jumped over. Every once in a while I would glance back and see it skip up maybe three meters high to clear something I'd had to work my way around.

It's one of those collie-sized Disneycorp models with pancake ears and flash-button eyes and a smile. It's the smile you remember after you've seen the little bastard hopping obstacles behind you with that crescent of white-painted teeth below those flashing eyes.

At first I thought it might have come out of a test program. When they introduce new models or modifications of old ones, they will often test them on random subjects. Hilda told me of a woman who was followed home by a murid that sat in her yard for a week because they forgot to recall it, and then something happened to it, it got a short and went out of control, and it hunted down and killed all the cats and dogs in that neighborhood. The police had to send out a couple of fast ursids to catch it and break it apart.

Well, after having circled the block, I stopped and looked at the murid, and the murid looked back at me from its thirty-meter interval, and I thought I had better get rid of it, so I could keep my visit to Dr. Grandgent a private matter.

The only way to stop a tracking murid is to enclose it. Slow it down somehow.

Once you're beyond its range, it has trouble picking you up.

What I did was to hunt around until I found what had evidently been some kind of garage—a one-story building with its roof still intact; long and low, all boarded up.

I pried loose a couple of boards and squeezed inside. It was filthy in there. Spiders and rats, cobwebs like curtains. Bat shit all over. In the corner a heap of bones, big bones. I followed the stream of sunlight from the open boards and went toward the far wall, counting my paces. Sure enough, when I got up to thirty, the murid showed up, stuck his beastly little head inside, then he slipped through the opening. When I moved one way, he moved, too—to maintain the track interval—and so step by step I was able to maneuver our positions until he was at the back and I was near the front. I didn't care to be in there with him, even though I was three times his size. There's something about those little fellows that makes my skin crawl. He was in the darkness, but I could tell where he was by his eyes and his smile. That's all I could see—the eyes flashing on and off, on and off, and the smile flickering as it picked up the flashes.

I squeezed my way outside and closed the opening by kicking the boards back in place and wedging them at the bottom with bricks. Then I jumped into the saddle of the single-wheeler and took off fast. In a few seconds I could hear him crashing and banging at the boards.

I am about two kilometers north of that spot. My guess is that he has broken free by now, but I doubt he'll be able to find me again.

Dr. Grandgent lives in a wreck of an old three-story mansion with broken windows and a sagging porch. The paint peeled off years ago, and wisteria is pulling the back rooms apart. In a manner of speaking, he doesn't live alone. He has a domestic felid that does the shopping and the cooking, guards the hens against rats, and tries to keep the underbrush from invading the place completely. It also plays chess with the old man in the evenings, if desired. (Dr. Grandgent ironically calls this robot "Professor McKay," after the chief design engineer of early-stage Wall construction—the George Washington, one might say, of the Atlantic Rampart system. I don't find this irreverence particularly amusing. It is one thing to ridicule bureaucratic nobodies like the Northeast crowd; it is quite another to mock a historic figure of the stature of Abraham McKay.)

My object in visiting Dr. Grandgent was to seek his counsel on the salinity phenomenon—and the failure of the surface sensor and backup systems to register it—since he knows as much as any living man about macroengineering and marine geophysics. This despite his retirement and virtual isolation for the past two decades.

What he told me I hesitate to record even here. It was very troubling.

Actually, I'm not sure I understood him completely—he has a way of hopping back and forth from one thing to another without warning, so when you think he's still talking about hydroperms, say, and discover he's jumped to tectonic flexogens, it leaves you mentally scrambling and plunging, trying to reconstruct his past meaning while not losing hold of what he's saying now. He was like that as a teacher—provocative but disorderly—and he's gotten worse.

He rambled and muttered and repeated himself, and instead of answering my questions he would hare off on some other subject. Once he fell asleep in his chair for a few minutes, snoring like a bear. I couldn't help wondering if he hadn't gotten a little senile after all these years alone in this wilderness. Which bothers me the more I think about it.

Can I trust his judgment?

Before I left, he promised to give me an introduction to one of his former prize pupils, Barney Dragomine, now a member of the Engineering Control Board.

This may not be worth anything in a practical sense. I doubt if a top executive like Dragomine would spare five seconds for a middle-grade administrator like me. At the most, he'd have a staff person see me.

My being on probation would make those people skeptical of anything I said, anyway.

It is mid-afternoon, and I am on the airbus flying back to Neptune. I can see two thin lines running across the horizon: Rampart and Wall. High above us are the fire-tracks of a dozen or so cargo shoots bound for Europe.

Before we land—it ought to be about ten more minutes—I want to set down a few of the things my old teacher told me while they are fresh in my mind.

We were in his study, and the felid had just mixed us some gin fizzes. Dr. Grandgent was in a relaxed mood. "The Wall isn't bad as a piece of engineering," he said. "It's a decent dike, as dikes go. If they'd kept to the original plan of putting sea walls around Boston and New York and the other ports, to keep them in business for another century or two until the glacial melt got too high—well, it would have worked out all right, Fowke, but the problem was they kept redesigning it, bigger and bigger, and the mania of size took hold of their brains until they lost all sense of feasibility and proportion. They decided they could do anything. They believed they could imitate the workings of Creation. But you cannot reproduce the living bone of earth. Canals crack and dams silt up. Rivers sink. Mountains rise and fall. They say the Wall will last a thousand years, give or take a hundred, but it's all guesswork now—the original studies haven't been updated—maybe they don't dare do it, Fowke, for fear of what they might find—and when I began raising these questions, they retired me—all of a sudden they decided my teaching and research services were no longer required!"

I didn't try to argue with him, even though I knew that much of what he said simply wasn't true. (We are assured, for example, that the base studies are updated continuously by an uninterrupted flow of information, recording the most minute alterations in heat, shock-vib, etc.) I just sat listening to him as he lolled back in his chair with his shirt halfway unbuttoned and his fingers picking through his white chest hair. "What man makes, Nature takes," he said. "You cannot build for the ages..." He went on disconnectedly talking about the drift factor and how Dr. Somebody's calculations had been proved wrong by Dr. Somebody Else, and when I tried finally to interrupt him—not to argue, but to soothe him down, because his color was flaming up, a sure sign of anger—he paid no attention to me.

He was almost shouting. "McKay and Gorton and the others back then knew enough to know they didn't know enough, but they went ahead anyway blowing their trumpets and beating their drums—McKay wasn't an engineer, he was a politician who turned into a power-mad fanatic—a pharaoh—the Wall was going to be his goddamned pyramid. That's what he wanted. You know he's buried inside the East Hatteras Scarp, don't you?" He went on like that for some time, while through the side window I caught glimpses of the felid outside swinging a sickle, and a good thing, too, because the creepers were all over that side of the house; some had sent green shoots through chinks in the wall, right into the room. ". . . can you imagine it, Fowke? A mammoth industrial engineering project bigger than anything done before, and it is carried along by a kind of crazy crusading enthusiasm that has nothing to do with engineering or economics—they were like children at the beach building sand castles—as if what they did would last forever—forgetting that the next tide would wipe it all flat—!" I tried again to get him onto a more peaceful topic, but he rolled right over me. "My great-uncle knew McKay's grandson," he said—I couldn't repress a grimace of revulsion at this viviparous reference—"and he had the same megalomaniac craziness. They finally had to lock him up. Pity they hadn't locked up old Abraham. He—the grandson—he wanted to build an Atlantic bridge. A bridge across the Atlantic! Wanted to dig a tunnel through Mount Everest, too! Why? Because it hadn't been done before! Because it would cost trillions and trillions of dollars and kill thousands of workers and be totally worthless—!"

I couldn't help reacting to this diatribe, since the Wall is practically a sacred thing to me, so I broke in to remind him of the Wall's huge energy yield, and the highly advantageous cost-benefit ratio of the farms and fishponds, etc., and I guess my tone must have had some hostility in it, because I was aware of a quick movement in the room, and all of a sudden that felid was right in front of me—a skinny construct about the size of a ten-year-old boy (if you can imagine a ten-year-old boy made out of tempered steel, with arms that reach the floor and have wicked-looking clawed grips on them). It didn't do anything. It just interposed itself between me and its master. I could smell its oil. I don't know what would have happened if I'd made a wrong move at that moment. Big as I am, that thing could have tossed me across the room. I shut up and sat still, and Dr. Grandgent laughed and thanked his learned colleague, as he put it, for the demonstration of protective loyalty, and he sent it back outside again.

After that I kept my voice down.

"They say you can judge a society by what it builds," old Grandgent said. "Some built for beauty, some for use. Look at the Egyptians. They built for death. And the Romans—they built to wash. The nomads didn't build at all. Maybe they were the smartest of the lot. Why build, when the good Lord has already fashioned the great things of this world? Not that I'm a believer, Fowke. It's just a manner of speaking." He let out a bellow that made me jump, but he was just summoning his felid in from the yard to mix another round. "As for us," the old man said, "we build toys, that's all we build. We're infantile monsters furnishing our playpen! The Wall? Don't make me laugh! It's a toy, too. A big toy—a complicated toy—but still just a toy . . ."

This tirade simply reinforced my impression that he'd let age get the better of him—and out of sheer obstinacy. He could have used the Juvenor like everybody else, but no, he had to let his brain and body wear down naturally—he's only about ninety, but looks a good thirty years older than that—just as he perversely insisted on living in this tumbledown house in the Baltimore wasteland like a barbarian, without a telemin or sonex or stimulator. Not even a simple comforter, as far as I could see, unless he keeps one in a closet. Why, essentially he lives like an excluded—barring the fact that he has a felid . . . and even here he isn't too well off, because although the one he has is versatile, it is far from defect-free. For instance, it failed to adjust its grip when it came in from clipping to mix our drinks, and broke quite a few glasses before it finally lightened up its touch. Later on I heard it out in the chicken house in back, plucking a hen for supper. It must have a snag in its track, because it plucked the hen *before* it wrung its neck. You never heard such squawks.

We were saying goodbye out on the porch. God, Baltimore gets hot in these mid-summer afternoons. I could see a turkey buzzard in the sky. Something had died out in the jungle and was rotting, and the breeze was telling us all about it. The porch had rot-holes in it. The honeysuckle was coming through; you could practically see it grow.

"Watch out for these people, Fowke," Dr. Grandgent said, blinking his rheumy eyes at me. "That fellow Matthews—he's a vindictive bastard once he's been crossed. I know damned well he was the one who got me retired with his scheming and finagling... and he's surrounded by toadies and incompetents and time-servers. Not a decent public servant in the lot!"

"They may not be worth much," I said, "but when they realize what's happening, they'll have to do something."

"They'll do something, all right," the old man said. He made a grimace. "But it may not be what you'd expect. Those slimy rascals!" I asked him what he meant by that—how could Northeast fail to take essential countermeasures once they finally became aware of the problem?—but Dr. Grandgent either didn't want to say or had lost the thread of his thought, for he just blew his nose over the edge of the porch and went back inside.

It was when I went down to where I had left the single-wheeler that I could see through a gap in the bushes out to the street—and there was the murid waiting for me. Those round ears and flashing eyes, that smile.

The little devil had picked up on me again... unless they sent out another one.

They all look alike.

JULY 24

Neglected to note that when I was in Baltimore I happened to pass an excluded colony back in the jungle behind the ruins of the old railroad station. I didn't see any of them—you hardly ever catch sight of one—just saw a line of smoke from their cooking fire and the path going into the bushes and some patches of color that might have been laundry. Most old seaboard cities have a few such colonies (limited in size by Interior Department regulations to no more than eighty individuals each, as larger groups might present problems of public order). According to official figures, there are about ten thousand excluded altogether in the East. Out West there are more, but they are kept in reservations for their own good, where they can have medical care, etc. The indigenous ones are pretty sickly and usually die off in their seventies. Half our span. And they say some people choose that life!

A quick trip across the Rampart and down to the Wall. The level of saline muck in the drainage trench seems about the same, but the area concerned has increased maybe two hundred meters in each direction. I transmitted a routine report on this saline spread—no more red flashes, I have decided—and later tried to call Dr. Matthews on the telemin, but he was in conference.

I noted the presence of the patrol ursid on top of the Wall right above me. He was stationary, looking down. He moved when I moved, staying above me.

This has never happened before.

JULY 25

Hilda was willing last night, so we spent an hour in our stimulators and emerged much refreshed. She is middleaged—in her mid-seventies—but has taken care of herself and is a fine figure of a woman, big and ample, with blond hair in braids becomingly coiled on her head. Her sensory equipment is in top working order. She volunteered for Shelf duty to get the vacation bonus, and is deputy control adjuster for track-robot services in this zone (not specialized ones like my felids, but the ordinary domestic and commercial ones, e.g., the murids who deliver groceries). Most of her work Hilda can do right in her bedroom via her terminal. She is an ardent neural painter. The living room walls in our house are covered with her works (which are too pale and formless with their muddy greens and yellows for my taste; I wish she had more clarity in her inspirations).

Being something of a romantic at heart, I have tried to get

a visual-type stimulator so I can see Hilda—or whoever it may be—while we are experiencing, but they are hard to get except second-hand. The manufacturers have discontinued the line. Hilda doesn't want one. She is a little prudish. When I told her about the time I stumbled across a couple of excluded who had strayed into the flatlands and were having sex behind a tree, she was not only embarrassed (to tell the truth, I was a little embarrassed myself, the thing was so blatant) but also offended, and wouldn't let me finish. Well, to me, the spectacle was ludicrous, frankly—the man and woman straining and groaning, with their legs all tangled together and their eyes bugged out. I couldn't help laughing and feeling a little sorry for them, deprived as they were of all but a minimal part of sensory contact, whereas with the stimulator we have total simultaneous involvement of the entire body surface plus the rhythmic rippler and the deep-excitation pulse, etc., which you can preset with the coital timer, with as many peaks and plateau pauses as you may desire.

Compared to the primitive and earthbound excluded, we soar like eagles, sexually speaking.

At the same time I must confess to having had a certain disquieting agitation watching those two people slamming against each other.

Once on impulse I took Hilda around the waist and gave her a direct mouth-to-mouth kiss—and she was furious and began lecturing me about germs and animalistic behavior, etc., and said if I wanted labial arousal, there was a place (the stimulator) for it. She even threatened to report me, although this was just in the heat of the moment. Naturally I apologized at once. She wouldn't speak to me for days, though; not that we talk much together. (I should note that we occupy the same house by assignment of the Neptune housing board; there is nothing personal involved. Neptune was built as a construction town in the middle years of the Wall project, back when there were couples and families, so it mostly consists of two-bedroom and three-bedroom houses, many in bad repair. Mine is one of the better places, as befits my rank.)

* * *

Bloom tells me he has heard of people who have experimented with flesh-contact sex. I can't believe everything Bloom says, but still this seems possible.

I wonder what it is like.

JULY 27

I finally got what I've been asking for all this past week—a telemax conference with Dr. Matthews. I got it only because I threatened to go up in person to Boston headquarters.

There is no telemax facility in Neptune. I had to drive to South Poseidon, where the Inland Valley Chamber of Commerce has one, and you'd think I was going to break it, the way they danced around me telling me where to sit and for God's sake not to touch anything or move, and under no circumstances to cross the white line.

I'd seen a telemax demonstration once down in Mississippi, but I'd never actually used one before. It is a special room, like a giant box, furnished (in this case) like an ordinary office, and when the thing is activated, you have the impression that you are right there with the other party in the same room, and that if you wanted to, you could reach out and touch his desk, or pick a flower from his vase, or walk over to his window and look down at the street. I've heard of cases where in the course of conferences people have forgotten about the white line and have strolled smack into a wall.

So there I was, apparently in the same room with Dr. Matthews, seeing him for the first time—and seeing, too, the view from his Boston office (which has a special terminal), a big wrap-around corner window overlooking Boston and Cambridge and the harbor flats and the Atlantis North plateau, with the Provincetown Rise visible as a bump on the horizon. The only jarring note was that my blue rug suddenly became a green rug halfway across the room.

Dr. Matthews is a skinny fellow with a pink complexion, plump cheeks, and a scraggly little mustache the color of wet sand. His eyes are small, and too close together. "I'm giving you five minutes, Fowke," he said with an unpleasant smile. "I'm a busy man, and I'm sure you are aware of the fact that I have twenty-three regional directors to supervise, of whom you are just one."

All the time I was talking, he ostentatiously read a report on his screen or did things like yawning and turning around in his swivel chair so his back was to me. I got so furious I felt like striding over to his desk and giving it a thump with my fist to get his attention—which would have put the Chamber of Commerce's telemax out of whack for some time to come, in view of my size, so maybe they were right to give me all those cautions about not moving.

I repeated everything I had reported to Dr. Matthews in my earlier messages, emphasizing the increasing indications of broad-front seepage and asking him to undertake a special field investigation, to alert other zones, notify all federal and state agencies, and make standby evacuation plans if they weren't already made, in case the situation started worsening at a faster rate.

Dr. Matthews held up his arm so I could see his wristwatch. "That's all, Fowke," he said with a petulant frown. "You've managed to waste some more of my time. Your assertions have absolutely no confirmation from the systems. Is that clear? Not a shred of evidence exists to support what you're saying."

"Send a field team down there. They'll find plenty of evidence."

"It would be pointless. And stupid. The systems themselves provide total and continuous monitoring already, and they are proof against the kind of human error and faulty judgment you've illustrated time and again with your hasty and misleading reports."

"If the systems say everything's all right, that means the systems are wrong."

He flushed from pink to tomato red. "The systems are never wrong! Never! I'm warning you, Fowke—!"

With that, he switched off his terminal, leaving me alone back in that telemax box in South Poseidon.

It is hopeless.

JULY 28

Tried three times to get through to Dragomine at Engineering Control Board headquarters in Omaha Down. His staff people insisted on knowing what it was about, and I couldn't risk saying. Dr. Grandgent's name didn't mean anything to them. The old man hasn't sent the message yet. Did he forget—or did he decide not to get mixed up in this?

I'm starting to think that the only way I'll be able to talk to Dragomine is by going out there.

JULY 29

A surprise caller at the office yesterday: an agent from the Atlantis North station of the Department of Interior Personnel Security. DIPS agents wear gray uniforms with square caps and black crossbelts, and you can tell them a mile off. Bloom took one look, turned pale, and popped an EZ pill into his mouth.

It turned out that I was the object of this visit.

The agent, name of Keller, was young—fresh out of Security School, I'm willing to bet—and had a puritanical expression, severe around the mouth, with a disapproving eye. I'd never seen her before, but something about her struck me as familiar; I couldn't think what it was.

At first I assumed that the reason for her visit was that episode in the airport manager's office when I accidentally split the counter.

It wasn't that.

It was about the Wall.

She was warning me to stop spreading rumors about Wall security that tended to undermine public confidence and might lead to fear and panic.

I was stunned; could hardly believe what she was saying. So ...the security problem at the Wall wasn't the salinity—wasn't the failure of the sensors and the backups—wasn't the spread of seepage.

It was me.

And who'd gotten the DIPS people after me—Dr. Matthews?

I told the agent as calmly as I could that I was doing my duty by reporting hydrodynamic phenomena to my superiors, and I would continue to do so, for otherwise I would be guilty of negligence, and as for the public, not a jot of information from my office had gone outside the chain of command (naturally I didn't say anything about Dr. Grandgent).

My voice must have gotten a bit loud, because she stepped back and replied in a rather strained way, telling me it wasn't in her competence to examine technical questions, her assignment was to give me the warning required by DIPS regulations.

I kept after her, insisting on knowing who had reported me, but she refused to tell me. "All our information is confidential, Commander Fowke," she said.

"I don't care about that. I've got the right to know who's telling lies about me."

"We never reveal sources."

I was starting to worry now, and began walking back and forth to relieve my feelings—"tramped" would be a better word, I guess, because the windows were rattling. They must have found out about my visit to Dr. Grandgent...but how? Through Bloom? That murid in Baltimore? Maybe there was an EAR link in Dr. Grandgent's house.

One thing that works in this country is personnel security. (System security may be another matter.) They may not know if the Wall is leaking, but they know what you ate for supper last night. I realized that I could be in serious trouble. One false step and they might bring me before a disciplinary board. Through the doorway I could see Bloom peeking like a freckled ghost around the edge of the codebank, listening for all he was worth.

"Look, Keller," I said. "Before you go back to your station, let me take you out to the Wall. You can see it with your own eyes and judge for yourself."

"It wouldn't mean anything to me. I'm not a technician."

"You don't have to have an engineering degree to know a ditch full of saline seepage when you see it. Have you ever seen the Wall?"

She shook her head, obviously rattled by my diametric reaction. She must be accustomed to people fawning and cringing and promising never to step out of line again, and here she comes up against a sizable character breathing defiance and making the floorboards shake.

"Every citizen ought to see the Wall, Keller. It is the greatest thing ever built in this country, and it is cited in practically every political speech and dedication address throughout the nation, but they don't bring the children out to see it any more, and they don't encourage tourism the way they used to, and now we've reached the point where even the people who live and work in the Valley, like you, can't be bothered making a little half-hour trip to look at it—!"

Well, I said all that and more, being worked up at the idea that the DIPS had sent this little ignoramus to slap my wrist, and she had never even seen the Wall. Never seen the Wall! This struck me as being typical of the slovenliness and neglect and lack of interest in important things that are ruining this country, and I guess maybe I said that, too, because she bristled up and began interrupting me, and after we'd had a couple of hot exchanges, she gave me a glare and marched out of the office with me behind her. I could see Bloom beyond the codebank practically in a faint.

I didn't want Agent Keller to leave in that angry frame of mind. I didn't care so much for myself—well, to be honest about it, I *did* care; suppose they sent me on tundra duty up north, or to some other place even more godforsaken than the Shelf?—but I was thinking, too, that the person who took my place might not be equipped to deal with what I am convinced is potentially major seepage out at Km 44–56. Would the next regional director have the guts to fight those drones up at Northeast?

I got in front of her and apologized for my bad manners and noisy ways and urged her to have a cup of coffee and take a little tour of our place—we have an interesting exhibit of marine fossils to show our occasional visitors—and as I do have a certain rude charm when I choose to use it, I managed to calm her down, although she still was sulky. I got the coffee-murid busy and escorted Keller through the hydrolab, etc., and introduced Bloom to her (he was still so nervous he wouldn't look at her directly). In a way, I pitied Keller. Security School must be no better than a prison. The way they drill them and program them up to the ears, they're practically like human felids. What kind of a life is it, going around snooping and warning people, telling them don't do this, don't do that? The worst part must be sensing the resentment people have for them. Anybody doing that rotten work must build up a lot of tension—and I bet they really unbutton in their private lives. I wonder if Keller goes on a tear now and then. She looks like she might have some pepper in her. She must be new at her job—she can't be more than thirty-five— and she doesn't seem warped yet. I got her laughing once. Again I had that strange sensation—a flash of something like recognition. Where had I known her before?

We were chatting in an almost friendly way when, like a fool, I said that, having been unable to get any action out of Northeast on the salinity problem, I intended bringing the question before someone higher up, maybe even a member of the Engineering Control Board itself.

That was a mistake. DIPS agents are steeped in the sanctity of going through channels. She flared up at once and began haranguing me. "Don't you realize, Fowke, that this would be a violation of organizational responsibility? Of fundamental social ethics?" She went on like that for some time, using words like "antifunctional," "insubordination," and "subversive."

I backtracked, trying to smooth it over—it would have been asinine of me to argue the point with a cipher like Keller. I even told her I really hadn't meant I would go outside channels, although I swore in my heart that I would take the chance—see Dragomine no matter what. What else could I do?

She was still peevish and suspicious when we got outside, walking well ahead of me—as if I was contaminated and might infect her—and then, just before she got into her duty machine, I did something I still can't quite justify to myself, it was such a violation of what you might call our unwritten moral code. I grabbed her hand. Many years ago a handshake was an acceptable courtesy, but of course nowadays it is taboo, since direct flesh contact of any kind is all but legally forbidden, such things having their historic roots in physical aggression and violence. She pulled back, shocked and outraged, but I had been too quick for her. That handshake—that touch—lasted for just a moment, but it was enough. My tactile recall is phenomenal. I knew right away.

"Excuse me," I said, "but what's your first name? Is it Julia?"

My question astounded her. She looked at me hard as she wiped her hand on her jacket, as if to rub off my touch.

"Is it?" I repeated.

She didn't reply. That was answer enough for me.

"I knew it was," I said. "We've met."

"No."

"I'm sure we have."

"I've never seen you before."

"We haven't seen each other—but we've met."

My meaning didn't get through to her right away. She gave me another hard look as she got into the machine, and then it hit her—the random scan!—and somewhat to my surprise, she blushed.

She blushed! My little DIPS agent, sweet Julia of the random scan—she blushed!

That was yesterday morning.

In the afternoon I went out to the Wall. It was raining hard—first real rain in weeks—and I realized as soon as I got near the trench that the runoff had raised the level to the point where the pumps began operating.

The rain was flushing out the trench—and the pumps were emptying it. The saline muck was gone—washed away—and with it vanished the visible evidence of seepage. It'll come back. The Deeps haven't sealed. I'm virtually sure of that. Nothing has changed. But when I saw the trench running with clear rainwater, I had a flash of panic, wondering if I was crazy, if I'd invented that salinity—and suppose Keller had come out with me, she'd have seen nothing to support my story!

The Wall hung above me, a deep dim gray sheet of rough

stone, rain-dark and slick and dripping. I looked up, the rain beating on my face, soaking my hair and beard. On the top was a patrol ursid, staring down at me. I watched him for a while, wondering if he'd move—I didn't like the implication that he might be tracked to pick up silhouettes on the ground—but I had to quit, because looking straight up like that with my head tipped back did something to my sense of balance, and I began to have the illusion that the Wall was starting to tilt, starting to lean, that it was about to come closing down on me like the night sky.

JULY 31

At this moment I am forty thousand meters above the Appalachians in a Boeing Airdart A–30 bound for Omaha.

It is an illegal trip—my probation status forbids me to travel west of Baltimore—but I am determined to talk to Dragomine at all costs—just go to his office and insist on getting in to see him.

What I did was to lift Bloom's trip-card from his wallet when he was in the wet room working on the pump relays.

Everything went smoothly. The box at the Baltimore airgate didn't bat an eye, so to speak, when I went through.

I won't get away with this, though. There are just too many damned controls.

We are crossing the Ohio River. It looks like a piece of string. Cincinnati is a smear down there.

Most other passengers are tourists. Few business people travel nowadays, the telemax having made it unnecessary.

We are starting our downglide. We are probably over Illinois, but the cloud cover blocks the view.

Scheduled to land in fifteen minutes at Omaha International, world's largest airport.

* * *

It is four o'clock in the afternoon, and I am sitting in the visitors' lobby of the Engineering Control building in Omaha Down, hoping to see Barney Dragomine. Every so often people pass through—top executives of the board, by the look of them (maybe including Dragomine himself, whom I've never seen)—but mostly I'm alone, the only person waiting. Under other circumstances, I might enjoy this place. It is a sort of garden, with plants and flowers and trees; a brook about two meters wide runs through the middle, and there are fish in it. Little birds are flying from branch to branch. I think they are mobiles.

All this is about nine hundred meters underground.

Tulsa and Wichita and Cheyenne have subterranean centers, too, but nothing on the scale of Omaha Down.

I'm using Bloom's name—had to, as I'm using his card—but sooner or later I'll have to identify myself, and there may be hell to pay, particularly when they find out I'm on probation. I'm not too presentable, either. I came in my field outfit, and I look as if I slept in it—pants wrinkled and jacket none too clean, boots needing polish.

It is quiet here. Just me and the flowers and flying-mobile birds under this big skydome with its fake clouds. There's even a little breeze. Not just an underground passage of dead air; it smells fresh, like the country, and makes you think of fields and forests. The whole thing is beautiful; spooky, but beautiful.

If they happen to have a storm programmed, I've got my raincoat handy. That's about the only thing I'd be ready for.

(Midnight)

In a real jam.

At a certain point I lost my head—acted on impulse to save myself—and made things worse.

It'll be Security Court for sure. There's nothing for me to do but get back to Neptune somehow—I'm in Des Moines now— and try to bluster it out.

I didn't see Barney Dragomine. I didn't even get close.

After I'd been sitting in the lobby for a good half-hour, I was called into an inner office to see one of the ECB staff directors, who turned out to be a strigid, one of those new super-tracks I'd heard about.

The office was furnished in a conventional way: carpeting, lamps, chairs, etc. Even a hat tree. Never having seen a strigid before, and finding the place apparently unoccupied, I was wondering where the staff director was, when I heard a soft, gentle woman's voice saying something like "Good afternoon, won't you please sit down?", which puzzled me, because I didn't know where it came from—where was this woman?—and I was looking here and there, until it dawned on me that the voice came out of that fat squat box on the desk. My first thought was that it was one of those antique intercoms, and the woman was in another office, speaking through it, but then, taking note of my perplexity, the strigid began explaining to me what it was.

If I'd been on ordinary business, I probably would have listened with considerable interest. I can't say I'm fascinated by technical innovations the way Bloom is, but I do like to keep up with new things. As it was, I was impatient to get in to see Dragomine, so I didn't pay close attention to what the strigid was saying. It wasn't much to look at, certainly. It had two lenses on it, big as saucers, with a little curved projection between them—the speaker—and up on top a pair of stubby bulges, probably antennae. Now and then the lenses would flick, imaging me, I suppose. The lasoid data source I couldn't see; probably came from above. What impressed me most about this thing was the voice, which—

(Had to break off to catch the Des Moines–Chicago glassway bus; only eight other people on it, the rest being murids—a dozen or so, sitting still as dolls in their seats.)

It's hard to describe that strigid's voice. A woman's voice, as I say—warm and kind, with a comforting authority in it, a friendly, soothing authority. You felt you could rely on it absolutely. Listening to it, I began to have the impression that I was in the presence of a genuine personality—not a real woman, exactly, not quite that, but something that was essentially human. Something that had heart and soul, intelligence and feeling.

I didn't understand at first that it wasn't just an administrative aide. It was a hypnogenetic control device—that's what it told me itself, in fact, but by then I was so befuddled that this information didn't mean anything to me. I was invaded by that voice—and by what lay beneath it, a sort of humming with a rhythmic beat to it, like a pulse, strong and dominating, which made me feel drowsy and submissive, the way you feel in a Juvenor, and then I wasn't aware of that any longer as a separate thing, for it seemed to have entered into me, become part of me. I was responding to the strigid's questions—who I was and why I had come there—or at least I suppose I was responding, because I had the impression that this exchange was taking place somewhere inside my mind; that I was listening not to words but to thoughts, and the thoughts were my own.

It wasn't just hypnosis. It was more than that. The damned thing worked into my brain, into my blood. I was ready to tell everything, I mean I was eager to do it, and when I say I wanted to tell everything, I don't mean just stealing Bloom's card and violating probation, I wanted to tell things like my kissing Hilda on the lips, and how I'd thrown a stone at a sparrow when I was a boy and killed it, and God knows what else was starting to boil up out of me, all mixed together, and I honestly don't know what I really said and what I thought I said.

Now, several hours later, as I'm gliding along the glassway—we're crossing the Davenport Arch at the moment—I have a little better grasp on what was going on between me and the strigid, or rather, between me and the actuation in strigid-form of the concept formulated by whatever cunning genius it was who designed that box.

I've recalled something written by the sociologist Dr. B. S. Glynn, which helped explain things to me—and I've found the reference on my pocket Librex. It's a passage from his *Essays on the Liberation of the Individual*, and I'll quote part of it here:

> The greatest social advance in our epoch—perhaps in any epoch in the history of the species—has been the victory over viviparity, Eve's curse. This has permitted population control, our triumph over the blind breeding urge that at one point threatened to smother humankind in its own sheer fecundity. But more important even than this: it has destroyed the family.
>
> The liberation of woman was the liberation of us all. No more father, mother, sister, brother. No more domineering possessive jealous "love," no more incestuous conflicts and degrading parent-child alliances; no more tender psyches wrecked by rebellion or submission.
>
> Still, although the family is virtually extinct among the civilized nations of the world, its memory remains deep in our racial awareness. It is an echo at the borders of our minds. Studies undertaken by Dr. Waldo Bailey of Tulane have indicated that

I won't bother copying any more of this out. Dr. Glynn's point is that we still have viviparous traces in our subconscious, and it was these which the strigid was reaching. I had a sick helpless feeling, as if things inside of me were being handled that shouldn't have been touched, and at the same time I was beginning to remember—well, not exactly remember, but recognize—recognize sensations I couldn't have ever had but which I knew were mine. It's upsetting even to think about this, upsetting to write it down. I was out of control, emotionally out of control. I had a terrible anguish—anguish mixed with a peculiar sort of exaltation, because I was eager and joyful, and yet also ashamed. Humiliated. Something in my—my what? My genes, maybe. A taint down there. Something was responding to that voice, that arterial pulsing. Some sick dormant cell had wakened. I was possessed by the sensation of being something pitiful and weak, like a child, in the presence of an ultimate authority, a human god,

arbitrary and all-powerful—is that what the family was like?—
the mother-voice joined to the father-drumbeat—all this from
that audio-technetronic construct spewing acousticephs at me—
and I was choking in a dizzy mix of emotions: loathing and
abjection, fear and adoration—

I was submerged in it, almost completely submerged. Part of
me stayed above the surface—buoyed up by my streak of diametric
contrariness, maybe—and I was aware in a distant way of what
was going on in that office—me sitting in front of a knobby
box—and I had a cloudy idea of what I seemed to be saying. Bits
and pieces are all I can remember.

The strigid knew I wasn't Bloom—I'd confessed to that—knew
I was Fowke, and knew why I'd come.

I managed to keep insisting that I wanted to see Dragomine.

"Do you really suppose, Mr. Fowke," said the strigid, "that a
man of Dr. Dragomine's standing would allow himself to be
drawn into an internal dispute in a subordinate agency?"

"It isn't that, really. It's—"

"We know what it is, Fowke. What we don't know is why
you're persisting despite the fact that all the evidence proves you're
wrong."

"That's not—not quite right. What I've seen myself—"

"Is it simply an honest error on your part, compounded by
your stubbornness and impulsiveness—or is there something behind it? Was this your idea, Fowke? Yours alone...?"

I didn't understand at first where things were heading. I seemed
to be drugged. The voice—the voice within me—I wanted to
follow it wherever it might take me. The anguish I felt—it must
have been guilt. I'd never felt guilt before. It was just a word to
me. I don't mean just being sorry for something—like killing the
sparrow—I mean *guilt*, which comes tearing up out of your guts,
a personal universal overwhelming sense of wrongdoing where
you are the center of a shameful evil world and your only choice
is to cleanse yourself, to liberate your soul of unbearable burdens
and beg forgiveness. To confess, as I said before. And more than
that: to involve others. I saw myself as the leader of a conspiracy.
I don't think I got as far as naming names—I hope not—but

names had begun to occur to me: Dr. Grandgent, Bloom, Caspar Tellis, who lives down the street from us; even Hilda. Julia, too.

I have no idea what would have happened if one of the birds hadn't gotten in there.

There was no door to the office, just a sound veil. The bird—the flying mobile—came straight through it and started beating against the far wall, fluttering up and down like a giant moth.

I was startled by it. The strigid paid it no attention.

"You were saying, Fowke—?"

"Excuse me. That bird—it's chipping the wall, and it's going to damage itself."

"Bird? What bird?"

"That one there. Why don't you call your murid in to catch it?"

"Don't talk nonsense," the strigid said, and its voice had an irritated edge to it.

"Can't you see it? Up there in the corner?"

"Fowke, you've been under strain, as is obvious from your actions—"

"You may not be able to see it, but you can hear it, can't you? It's making a hell of a racket."

"Let's get back to the subject at hand, Fowke."

"But the bird—"

"There is no bird here!"

I couldn't help it, I laughed. It was too much, this strigid being programmed for God knows how many millions of complex probabilities, everything foreseen and accounted for, everything except something as piddling and unlikely as a flying mobile getting untracked, and the strigid didn't see it, *couldn't* see it, and was getting furious with me for insisting it was there. No bird; no salinity. And so I sat there snickering and chuckling. Couldn't keep it in.

"We're warning you, Fowke," said the strigid. "You have a lot to explain...!" But the magic was gone. I was liberated from that voice. The bird was banging and scraping at the ceiling. Some of its feathers were bent; the paint was skinning off.

The strigid, annoyed, had lost its patience. "You're wasting time, Fowke! Answer the questions!"

"I'll bet Dragomine could see that bird," I said—a mistake, evidently, for it seemed to infuriate the strigid. "You'd better cooperate, Fowke!" it said in a harsh tone. "Otherwise I'll have no choice but to take appropriate action to deal with your intrusion! Do you want me to call the guards—?"

I realized that the situation was deteriorating and knew I'd better leave with as much dignity as I could muster and try to reach Dragomine some other way later on. What I actually did was the worst possible thing, but it was a nightmare, with that mobile clattering against the wall and the strigid squawking at me, and I was still churned up and befuddled by my regressive reactions to the mother-voice, and also worried that at any moment a couple of ursids might rush in to haul me away and maybe twist my arms off in the process, so instead of acting rationally, I gave way to panic.

I grabbed the strigid off the desk (it was surprisingly light), wrapped it in my raincoat, and went out fast through the sound veil into the lobby. All I could think of was that I had to silence that thing—break its lasoid link—and nothing better occurred to me.

Why the ursid at the front entrance didn't stop me I'll never know. I went right past it. The strigid was still screeching, muffled by the raincoat—or at least I thought it was screeching, using its residual charge, but maybe that was just my imagination.

I went out among the late-afternoon strollers looking into the windows of the stores along the Underway. I got onto the first moving ramp I came to, then got off and walked, then took another ramp. Up, down; it didn't matter. I had no idea of where I was or what to do. What a mess. Here I was, blundering around in Omaha Down with a ten-million-dollar strigid under my arm, looking for a way out.

I was in no mood to appreciate the city's famous spectacles: the sunshafts, the rainbow lights, the air bridges. My thoughts were fixed on that strigid humming inside my raincoat. Was the damned thing sending out distress signals? I was tramping and panting, wiping perspiration out of my eyes with my free hand. In the middle of Monument Square Under, I sat on a bench to rest. The place is huge. You could put a cathedral at the far end, and it would look like a bird cage.

There were crowds there, but the sounds of footsteps and voices were sucked up and dispersed by the vastness of the square; all I heard was silence. Looking around, I had the impression of being sunk in the sea—the light changes, sometimes it is greenish, sometimes it's gold—but when I raised my eyes to the glasstic walls that tower up out of sight, I felt I was rising into the clouds.

There was an up-ramp at one corner. I could see its zigzag track shining inside the glasstic. I headed toward it past the water statues and the clusters of pigeon-mobiles strutting among the tourists feeding them popcorn (which these birds actually gobble down; guess they have to be emptied at the end of the day).

I was so anxious to get on the ramp and so worried about the strigid—what was I going to do with it? get rid of it, yes, but how?—that I almost walked into a police patrol that might very well have been looking specifically for me: two uniformed ursids with sandbag mitts on them beside a police sergeant (human) who had a corkgun on one hip. I was partly screened by some tourists. Big people, Alaskans, to judge by their accent. I mingled with them and got past the patrol. We came to some public comforter booths, and I lost no time slipping into one of them (a tight squeeze, with that bundled strigid wedged against me). I was too agitated to get much calm out of the comforter—it was just a place to hide, and a good one, too, for it is a kind of sanctuary; no one will intrude on you there. I could feel the warmth of the cuddlers and rockers, but I couldn't relax for an instant, being intent on keeping one eye at the slit to watch the ursids and the cop, wondering which way they'd move, if they moved. The murmurer reminded me of the strigid, and I switched it off.

Finally the patrol shifted off a different way. I left the booth and hurried over to the up-ramp, took the rapid ascent belt.

It was sundown in Omaha Up. The old city is sleazy and tumbledown, populated largely by low-grade service supervisors and elderly people who for some reason don't care to live underground. The Hilton Hotel is a felid station, and the Masonic Manor is an airbus hangar. There is a colony of excluded enclosed by a high wire fence behind the old courthouse. I caught a glimpse of two of them as I hurried by—a male and female standing at the fence side by side, looking out. They were holding hands. It gave me a strange sensation. So did the fence. I was bothered by that—I hadn't known that was done anywhere—but I guess it may be necessary to keep them out of trouble.

I caught a Council Bluffs car on the Farnam Street line and got off at the river stop to see if I was being followed. Nobody got off with me. For the moment I was alone on the platform. Night was coming fast, but the lights weren't on yet. Looking over the railing, I could see the Missouri running broad and dark. There were points of light down there: channel-markers. I could smell the river—wet and dirty, moving fast.

I didn't wait any longer. Lifted the strigid over the railing. Shook it out of my raincoat. I thought I heard a noise from it as it tumbled, a sort of hoot. Then it was gone. I didn't hear it hit.

AUGUST 1

It was four o'clock in the morning when I got back. Hilda wasn't there—she's attending a cybernationist convention in London—and the house was empty. I couldn't get to sleep, so I took a shower and got into the stimulator, setting it for a rubdown. Emerged energized, but still worried, wondering what they would do to me. Suppose they found the strigid?

At nine o'clock I went to the office and found Bloom there, to my surprise. It wasn't one of his duty days (we work the twenty-hour week, like everyone else), and he is a stickler for the rules.

"They're looking for you," he said.

"Who?"

"That DIPS agent. She called yesterday, and said she was coming here today. And Northeast has been flashing you."

Bloom was agitated. He kept cracking his knuckles and swallowing. "You'd better answer them," he said. "Dr. Matthews himself was on the board last time."

"The hell with Dr. Matthews."

Bloom sucked in his breath. "Be careful," he said. "You're in enough trouble without making it worse."

I knew he was right—Northeast was probably monitoring with the EAR link—but I was angry and worried, and I didn't give a damn. "The hell with them all," I said. I shouted it. I was pacing around the place, with Bloom scuttling behind me, keeping his distance. The office felids were busy as usual at their counters, checking the flow of data from the stream-gauges and windpoints, etc. From the labs I could hear the clicks and gurgles of the analyzers.

I headed for my office. The door was closed. I put my thumb against the print-register, but nothing happened.

"What's wrong with this?" I snapped at Bloom.

"They've suspended you," he said. I turned to face him. He edged back. "Don't blame me, Commander. They did it yesterday. Dr. Matthews ordered it."

"And they changed the lock-print?"

Bloom's face flushed pink. His freckles were like measle spots. "I'm—they made me—I'm acting director now. Until you're cleared."

I glared at him, but said nothing.

He mustered up a little courage. "You'd better give me back my trip-card. You had no right to take it. They thought I gave it to you, and I had to explain—"

I turned and gave the door a tremendous kick. The lock gave. The knob gave, too, and part of the paneling disappeared. I did it out of sheer rage. I didn't want to go in there. I pulled Bloom's trip-card from my pocket, tore it in two, and flung the pieces at him. I was stamping and yelling, partly because of the pain in my foot from that ill-considered kick. Bloom hastily backed away. I went past him, cursing, limped outside, got into my duty machine, jammed it into high gear, and went off at a tear, heading for the Rampart road.

It was one of those muggy summer mornings in the Shelf valley when you seem to be breathing your own breath over and over again, and it gets thicker and sourer all the time. The leaves on the trees were limp. There was a sort of sweaty fog lying in the low places.

As I drove up the Rampart, the air lightened and cleared. On the ridge it was cooler. I stopped there. What was I going to do? The flasher on the panel was blinking—that would be Northeast—but I ignored it. I also ignored the voice that soon came screeching out of the speaker. "Fowke? Fowke? Do you hear, Fowke? Acknowledge at once!" It sounded like Dr. Matthews. I could imagine him up in his fancy Boston office, getting red in the face as he yelled into his MK. "Report immediately, do you hear? Acknowledge me!"

I simply turned the main panel off, got out of the machine, and stood looking at the valley. The fog curled and smoked down there, drifting across the roads and sluicing between the houses and the trees like a phantom sea.

I turned the other way, east. There was the Wall.

As I let my gaze rest on its horizontal mass, I felt calmer; it was as if something of the Wall's solidity and strength entered into me. I stood there breathing the ocean air that rode in over the Wall and across the flatlands, and I wondered what suspension would mean. I might be placed under strict probationary control. House arrest, in effect. Or even detention in the Atlantis North security center, pending disposition of my case.

Whatever happened, I would certainly be denied access not only to my office and my terminals and my records—I would be denied access to the Wall.

This could be my last chance to go there. And by now the Deeps would have sealed if they were going to seal at all. Which I doubted.

I had to know that. Had to see it. I got back in the machine and drove down the seaward side of the Rampart toward the flatlands. The road curves through stands of birch and chestnut and oak, passing a scattering of empty houses abandoned by people who transferred west, and old picnic grounds that haven't been used since the last tourists came. The trees have been tilted inland by the ocean winds, and the houses are being invaded by weeds.

I reached the bottom and gunned the machine across the flat-lands, breaking veil after veil of mist. The Wall seemed to rise up the nearer I got—a granite cliff sliding toward the sky, its morning shadow dark along the embankment.

I skidded to a stop at the trench, jumped out, and went to the edge.

The brine was back, all right. I went down the facing stones and waded into it. Two days before, the pumps had flushed it out, and now here it was again, almost as high as it had been before.

That meant it was coming in faster.

I dipped my finger into it, tasting it just to be sure. Salty.

If the flow was greater, then the seepage front had to be wider. How wide?

I knew I could get a rough idea from the top of the Wall, so I drove to where the climb was and started up. The rungs were slippery with the morning damp. I didn't have my gloves; I could feel the rusty metal biting into my hands. My boots were heavy with muck from the trench. Lack of sleep had sapped my strength. I was short of breath; my shoulders ached; the sweat ran down my back, down my face. I had to shake my head to clear my eyes.

Halfway up, I heard someone calling from below. I looked down over one shoulder. A figure in gray was standing on the hood of a duty machine parked beside mine—someone with a bullhorn. Her voice—it was Julia Keller—came booming up. She was ordering me to climb back down. I didn't waste my breath yelling back at her. I couldn't have gone down even if I'd wanted to. I had to get on top and rest—and have a look along the trench.

It must have taken me another twenty minutes to climb the rest of the way, with Keller's voice squawking at me, and the wet heat pouring over me, and gnats in my eyes, and my shoulders and legs burning with fatigue. When I got to the top, I lay there exhausted. The sky was swimming over me, thick as butter. I couldn't hear Keller now, and figured she had given up and gone away.

It was when I was strong enough to sit upright that I remembered the patrol ursid and took a quick scan north and south with the binoculars. He wasn't in sight. I began walking north, pausing now and then to look down at the trench, checking the metal kilometer markers. It was low tide. On the ocean side, the breakwater reared up like a whale's back, humped and slick and dark and spotted with gulls. Between the breakwater and the Wall, the water churned and frothed, the trapped waves beating.

The northern limit of the seepage had been Km 56. Now it was past Km 58. I couldn't tell how far beyond that.

I turned and headed back. From a distance I saw something on top of the Wall. At first I thought it might be the ursid—and then I realized it was Keller.

She had climbed up after me and was resting on her hands and knees. She wasn't just exhausted. As I got nearer, I could see she was dazed by fear. The Wall is something like thirty meters thick at the embankment level but tapers to a five-meter width at the top. To a novice climber, that feels as narrow as a plank.

"Keller—what the devil are you doing up here?"

She looked up at me, her gaze unwillingly rising. The sight of me standing on that dizzy rim of stone must have made her quail with height sickness. She'd lost her cap in the climb. There were streaks of moss and sand on the front of her uniform.

"I'm arresting you, Fowke," she said.

"Arrest? Don't be ridiculous."

The arrest card had fallen out of her breast pocket, but as she reached for it, a finger of wind flipped it over the ocean side. She watched in dread as it sailed out and down, dwindling until it was a red patch on the water.

She shuddered and closed her eyes. I remembered my first time on the Wall. It is like no other high place, because the ocean stands so visibly and enormously higher than the land on the other side, creating such a terrifying effect of imbalance that you feel the whole thing will tumble over landwards, that it *is* tumbling, in slow motion. Looking down is frightening, but looking up—if there are clouds blowing across—can be almost as bad.

Most of the Wall walkers killed were up for the first time.

"So what are you going to do with me?" I asked sarcastically. "Handcuff me and carry me down?"

She squinted cautiously around, closed her eyes again.

The problem, I realized, was my problem. How was I going to get *her* down?

"Do you have a minitel?" I asked her. She shook her head. She'd left it in the machine down below. We had no way to call a patrol craft, unless I left her alone while I climbed down.

But suppose the patrol ursid showed up in the meantime?

"You made a fine mess of things, climbing up here," I said angrily. "Did you think I was trying to escape? Don't they teach you to use your brains? Couldn't you see it was dangerous?"

"I'm not afraid," she said defiantly, but she didn't move—she couldn't—and she was pale and trembling. I had to admire her spirit, or whatever blind bureaucratic obedience to duty made her clamber up that trail of rusty rungs to serve me with that damned order.

I squatted down beside her. "You're going to have to pull yourself together, understand? I can't carry you down. Some of the rungs are loose as it is." One of her hairbands had snapped, and strands of black hair were blowing across her face. "The first thing you've got to do," I said, "is sit up. Then open your eyes— open them all the way—and look in a horizontal direction. Look at something close first. Look at your hands. Then try to get to your knees..."

The clouds were drifting low. Mist came steaming up. I couldn't see more than a hundred meters in any direction. The flatlands disappeared in the haze, and the Rampart was hidden. I could hear the gulls screaming out at the breakwater, but I could no longer see them. The Wall was a shelf of stone in a luminous sea of fog.

I kept working with her—talking to her, encouraging her, bullying her. She got to her knees, to her feet. She stood there, terrified.

"Now take a step," I told her.

"It makes me dizzy," she said queasily.

"You'll get over that. Don't give in. You've got to fight it. Take that step."

She took a step toward me wavered.

"Now another one."

"I can't."

"You'd better try. How do you think we're going to get down?"

She took a second step, a third, a fourth, with me facing her, backing as she advanced.

"That's better," I said, but then she made the mistake of glancing over the ocean side into that gulf of mist, and she tottered, reached out for me as I stepped up to grab her. She staggered against me; I caught her, held her. I could feel her trembling. Her head against my chest, her heart hammering. It was a strange sensation. Strange and strong. She tipped her head back; we stared into each other's eyes. I felt a little dizzy now myself, but not from the height. Her face was oval, her skin olive, her eyes a fierce light blue. All this happened in an instant—her losing her balance, my catching her and holding her—and I was bewildered. Why should this accidental closeness—the brief contact of our bodies—have had such a powerful effect? We were hardly strangers, in a physical sense. Through the Telesex random scan, we had already had an incomparably more profound sensual experience—the customary total corporeal electrosexual exploration. There had been hardly a pore we didn't poke into, so to speak. And yet here we were, shaken and perturbed by this chance physical encounter, this touching of our hands, our eyes, the warmth we felt from each other's bodies. We broke apart as if in guilt, amazed by the unexpected force of feeling. But *what* feeling?

We broke away, as I say, but she had to have my support, so with some misgivings I began to walk her along the top of the Wall, one arm across her shoulders. She held me around the waist. We must have looked like a courting couple out of some antique film. That sensation returned, though—at least it did to me—and I still couldn't understand it. Was it a sort of protective tenderness? Simply the strangeness of contact? I remembered the impulse that had made me kiss Hilda that one time, how outraged Hilda had been.

Touching is regarded as regressive and primitive, like eating with your fingers or spitting in public. Animals touch; the excluded touch. We don't. In lifecamp and lifeschool, we as children were made to understand that touching is rooted in viviparity. It is the first step toward physical aggression and domination. We learn to respect the bodily integrity and independence of others. To satisfy sensorimotor needs, we use the comforter and the stimulator. In just a few generations, we have all but eliminated the crimes inevitable in a society which permits physical contact: rape, incest, child abuse, etc.

I know all that. I believe in it. Nonetheless I got a peculiar sensation walking Julia along the top of the Wall in the ocean mist, feeling her arm around my waist. I didn't want to stop. I don't think she did, either. She was walking well now. She didn't have to have my support. But she didn't withdraw her arm, didn't pull away. We had come together out of need; now the need was gone, and we were experiencing other feelings—a sort of longing, mixed with sensations of sin. It was a forbidden thing—not exactly forbidden, but certainly outside the accepted pattern of social behavior. *Thou shalt not touch.* It is all but written into law. Even so, we touched; we touched.

All this time, to distract her from her height sickness, I was talking to her, telling her about the seepage and the inexplicable failure of the sensors and the backups—now the Deeps, too, had proved incapable of sealing—and how my efforts to make the higher-ups see the truth had gotten me into trouble. Was she listening? I mean, did she understand? I don't know if I was making any sense to her. I was talking just to be talking. What I was aware of was our touching—and the fact that this paragon of duty, this embodiment of the law, this slender little DIPS agent, capless with her hair swirling in the soft damp Wall-top winds, was clasping my waist tightly, her head against my shoulder. We were in a kind of trance, lost track of time, of distance.

"Do you think you can climb down now?" I asked.

"Yes, I'm all right. I can do it."

We turned around to start back—and saw the patrol ursid coming at us through the mist.

He had passed the point where the rungs were. We were blocked.

I stared at the ursid, stupefied. I'd forgotten about him. He came trundling along thick and low, points of moisture glistening on his shaggy coat of weatherproofing, his shining lenses wet. Julia backed off, pulling my arm. She'd never seen an ursid like that before. I hadn't told her about him—she'd had enough to worry about without that.

"Get down," I said. "Lie flat." The ursid was some fifty meters away. Could we get under his track-sight? She was slow to move. I had to pull her down. "Keep your head low," I told her. "Don't look up."

Once we got down below gull-level, the ursid lost our silhouettes and hesitated. I prayed the bastard would turn around and go back. He didn't. He kept coming. He hadn't reached his patrol turn-point. If we squirmed toward the edge, out of his path, would he go past us?

I could hear him creaking as he came nearer. It sounded like asthmatic breathing. His pads scraped rhythmically across the rock. Julia couldn't stand it. She jumped up. "Run, Fowke— run!" The ursid caught her silhouette, increased his pace. I scrambled to my feet and ran after her. It was pointless. We could outrun him, but only for a while. We would tire. He wouldn't.

We didn't go far. She slipped on the wet stone and fell to her knees. I stopped and turned to face the ursid, who was drumming across the last few meters that separated us. I'd never been so close to him before. I noticed every detail, his round head streaked with rust-colored lichen, his shoulder casings spotted with salt rings. Beneath were his front grabs—and they were beginning to unfold. I tore off my jacket with the crazy notion of throwing it to him. Let him grab that.

He was rising on his haunches in front of me, ready to strike. I flung the jacket over his head. For the moment he was disoriented. When he grabbed for me, he grabbed low. I jumped to one side. He came past me, ripping at the jacket, going straight for Julia, who crouched where she had fallen, dazed. I rushed after him, kicking at his hindquarters, trying to turn him over, trying to shove him to one side. He swung around, lashing out with one clawed grab—the other was rending and pulping my jacket, popping the buttons like walnuts. He grazed me. My left sleeve hung in shreds; my arm was slashed from shoulder to elbow. He reared up, grabs spread, ready to clamp me. For a moment he was balanced on his haunches, his undercarriage exposed, and I launched myself at him feet first. Hit him square. He tilted over backwards, his grabs flailing, and immediately spun over to right himself—rolled the wrong way. He was too close to the land-side edge, and he went over. I saw one grab biting into the granite as he fought to clamber back. Chips of stone went spitting up. Then he lost hold, vanished. I crawled over to look down and saw him smashed there on the embankment, broken in pieces, one grab still snapping air.

PART TWO

AUGUST 3

I am sitting on my bunk at the Atlantis North detention center, waiting for arraignment, with twenty-four stitches in my left arm. A murid stands outside my cell, watching me. Each occupied cell has one. At the end of the corridor is the felid-in-charge. Every thirty seconds—I've timed it—my murid gives off a little squeak. Reporting to the felid, I guess.

The cell is well furnished: comforter, Vidipix, wash basin, etc. They let me keep my pocket Librex and the micropen, so at least I can continue making this record.

I will be tried—assuming I am arraigned—in Security Court, which has operated under court-martial regulations since the Eleventh Hoover Commission governmental reorganization, in '33. The difference from the civil system is only in form, and the rights of the accused are fully respected—this is what my lawyer assured me today at our first conference. He is a big beefy Army captain named Foster Beeney, and seems to be competent. At first he was doubtful about the kind of presentation I wanted him to make, but in the end he promised to do everything in his power to see that I got both justice and satisfaction. He told me he felt sure the judge would dismiss the case. My impression is that at worst I can expect a suspension from duty for a few months. "You've got nothing to worry about, Commander," Captain Beeney told me as he left.

Luckily for me, that patrol ursid sent out an automatic call signal before it went over the edge of the Wall, so that within twenty minutes a hover craft showed up to take us off. I don't know how we would have gotten down otherwise. I'd lost blood and felt weak. I told Julia to climb down and get help, but she wouldn't leave me.

The hover flew us to the Neptune hospital, where they sewed up my arm and gave me some plasmite. I must have drunk a liter of the stuff. Then they released me. I was expecting Julia to do something—after all, she'd gone out to the Wall to serve that arrest order—but she didn't, she looked the other way when the doctor was voxing his case record. They called a taxi for me. Just before I got in, Julia did an unusual thing. She put her finger against my wrist. Touched me, right there in front of the doctor and the nurse. I imagine they were taken aback by that, but I wasn't looking at them. I was looking at her, looking into those eyes the color of the morning sea, feeling that fleeting touch, her finger brushing my skin. "Sleep well," she said. Why didn't she arrest me? Why the touch? I couldn't stop wondering, couldn't stop thinking about her. That night—it was night before last—just as I was getting ready to go to bed, I had an inspiration and went to the stimulator and checked the random scan.

There she was, waiting. She didn't list her name this time, but she didn't need to. I remembered her tactile energy readings, and I know she remembered mine, because when I ran them across the board, she didn't hesitate; she acknowledged and accepted at once. I couldn't zip myself into the electroexcitor envelope fast enough. In fact, I neglected to punch in any of the usual settings—the rippler, the erectile extensor, etc.—but we didn't need any of that, we were so aroused. Never with Hilda or any of the others can I remember such a powerful experience. I felt the fire of it burn through me again and again, wave after wave, beating deeper each time, dissolving me.

And yet I had a sensation of failure, I mean I felt that we were missing something, that there was a height we fell short of, like the final peak of a mountain hidden in the mists, when you're so high up you're dizzy with the exhilaration of it, and yet you know you haven't gone all the way.

What I wanted was visual contact. I wanted to see her. I wanted to know that she saw me, too. And more than that—I might as well admit it—I wanted to be with her, I don't say to touch, that might be going too far, it seems almost a wicked thing, although I will never forget the sensations I had on the Wall when I held her in my arms... but to be in her presence. To be close. If not to touch, at least to see. For the first time in my life I felt the overpowering desire to be with another person, and it was confusing, because I know that in the stimulator we achieved the ultimate closeness technosexology is capable of providing, and yet I was aware of the emptiness that divided us—me there in Neptune, and she in her cubicle in the DIPS barracks in Atlantis North, three hundred kilometers northeast of me—and it was like a barrier between us, this apartness, this hollowness of space.

I wonder if she felt this, too.

The lead news on the Vidipix this noon was that the U.S. has gone under the fifty-million population mark—just announced by President Leavit from the White House in Denver.

It's hard to imagine what life must have been like back when there were five or six times as many people. The old films of jammed sidewalks in the cities, of rush-hour crowds cramming into subways and buses, don't begin to convey how suffocating life must have been then. Even the jails were crowded. I don't think I could have stood that.

The morning after I fought the ursid on the Wall, two agents came to arrest me, with an ursid in attendance (to quiet me, in case I made trouble). One of the agents was Julia, cold and distant. She wouldn't even look at me while the other one, a man, read me the order. I rode in back with the ursid; they were up front. Nobody spoke. They didn't, and I decided not to. What could I say to her, with that fellow there? It was a long, lonely ride on the glassway, I can tell you, and when we got to Atlantis North, it was the other agent who booked me in. Julia stayed in the background, and I couldn't catch her eye.

I remember her as she was then—pale and stiff in her gray uniform, her cap set straight to the millimeter. Contained, that's how she looked. Bound in, restrained, repressed—unless it's just my imagination that there is something in her fighting to break free, something wild, something reckless. Why else would she have climbed the Wall? Why else would she have sought me on the scan?

AUGUST 5

My pocket Librex gives me access to the Library Bank, so I can read as much as I like in order to pass the time, and I've been amusing myself flipping through some of the old classics: Tolstoy, Shakespeare, Proust. There was a time when these things were forbidden because of the supposedly harmful effect they would have as viviparous propaganda. I was a toddler when the ban was lifted, the government having decided that it no longer made any sense.

Many passages are beautiful, but the point of view is ridiculous. How could people have believed in such things? *Hamlet* is a ludicrous story to modern readers liberated from family life. A character who has a "father" and a "mother" is enough to put you off in the first place, and then when they go around killing one another and plotting revenge—well, the whole thing is preposterous and totally false to the way human beings actually think and behave. As for *Anna Karenina*, all that aggressive passion is monstrous. The only decent passage in the book is at the end, where she jumps under the train.

AUGUST 8

I don't know how many other inmates there are here. Maybe a dozen. Certainly not more than twenty. Every now and then I glimpse one of them walking along the corridor under escort. We are kept apart and do nothing in common. This suits me fine—and probably suits the others, too.

In general, the treatment isn't bad. The food is first-rate, even though it must be laced with EZ concentrates to control worry levels. Each night the murid wheels in a stimulator for me to use. It's supposed to give you the feeling of sensory freedom, but it has limited settings and no outside scan, so clearly all you get are Telesex stock models.

Still, I can't complain. I lack nothing. Nothing much. In fact, it has occurred to me that life here is little different from life anywhere.

AUGUST 10

Prisoners—or detainees, as in my case, since I haven't been arraigned yet—are allowed to have parcels sent in from the outside, so I sent word to Hilda to pack up the contents of my top drawer, although most of the stuff I don't need here. She sent me the package without a note or message, and of course she didn't come in person. I didn't expect her to. The American way of life is based on respect for the individual, and nonintervention in the emotional and social problems of others, as this tends to create interpersonal stress. Any such gesture by Hilda would undoubtedly have set up expectations in me and guilts and resentments in her, which would have amounted to a mutual invasion of privacy, and in a small way it would be like mourning the dead, which is forbidden by our moral code. So I respect Hilda's decision.

I would like to see Julia, though.

I skipped lunch in order to avoid the EZ dosage and check my anxieties. Sure enough, by four o'clock in the afternoon, I experienced a palpable rise in my worry level.

The saline front at the Wall must be at least thirty kilometers long by now.

But is it happening only down at Baltimore Canyon? Is it conceivable that there are seepage points elsewhere? At Fundy and Hatteras and the East Georgia Plate?

Dr. Grandgent talked about *system refusal*. To the extent I understood him, I remember nothing that would exclude multiple independent seepage, except then I was thinking only of the Canyon—what I had seen myself—and it wasn't until today that it occurred to me that the same thing might have started in other regions.

What a fool I was. I should have kept my head and done some quiet checking with other regional directors; no, instead I had to go off half-cocked and get myself in trouble.

In my present situation I am powerless.

AUGUST 16

Arraignment today.

At nine o'clock in the morning I was taken under guard out of the detention center and transported to the court, a couple of kilometers away.

Atlantis North is bleak and grim, a military base sitting on the tip of the Provincetown Rise, overlooking a wasteland of sand and rock. The heat is terrible—and the Atlantic winds gusting from the east send sand flailing in. When those winds blow, the filters can't handle the stuff. It gets into your skin, your hair, your food. Track-robots are sealed, but it gets into them, too, and they have a short life up here. There is a heap of metal carcasses behind the detention center.

The tribunal is a windowless tower just south of the Boston glassway entrance ramp.

The magistrate, a colonel, sat behind the high bench in a small gray courtroom. The only patch of color was the flag with its stripes and fifty-two stars. I had hoped Julia would be present— she was the arresting officer—but she wasn't. No one was there except for the magistrate, me, the major who was the prosecutor, my lawyer Beeney, the clerk (a felid), and the ursid-at-arms by the door. You'd think Dr. Matthews would have sent somebody from Northeast to put in a good word for me, at least to cite my commendations, but no, there wasn't a soul. I can rot in this hole for all they care.

The proceedings didn't last long. The prosecutor got up to describe me as an unruly and reckless element whose actions tended to disrupt the proper functioning of a small but vital link in the systems on which our nation depends, etc., and therefore I was not only incompetent but potentially a menace.

To which Captain Beeney didn't object. I was thunderstruck. He merely told the magistrate I had meant well and threw me on the mercy of the court, so to speak. That was all. The sabotaging bastard! I'd thought we'd agreed that he would lay out the whole story: the Wall, the seepage, my reports to Northeast, everything—the reasons *why* I did what I did, but obviously my lawyer was in cahoots with the rest of them to smother any reference to the Wall and to hustle me through a farce of an arraignment, giving merely the appearance of due process. When I got up myself, red in the face and sweating with anger, to take up my own defense, the colonel began beating with his gavel and ordered the ursid to remove me if I didn't keep quiet. I didn't want to be dragged out of there, so I closed my mouth.

They ran through the rest of the comedy as fast as possible. I was arraigned for various misdemeanors and regulation violations: probation breaking; theft (Bloom's card); destruction of federal property (presumably the Wall ursid, as nothing was said about the strigid); and several other charges I didn't pay much attention to.

The whole thing took maybe twenty minutes. I was remanded for trial on the September docket.

AUGUST 19

I have become increasingly concerned about my legal situation and have dismissed that fat fool of a captain. In his place I have a civilian lawyer from Boston, a tall spare fellow named Hooper Gleason, but even with him I don't find myself much encouraged, especially since his reaction to what I tell him about seepage at the Wall is one of polite disinterest. I don't think he believes me.

AUGUST 20

What will happen to me if I lose my case (as seems likely)? I've thought about this a lot, going over the range of disciplinary punishments. I wouldn't care for any of them—a transfer, for instance—and I've decided to ask for retirement on half-pay. I could scrape along well enough.

There's a retirement center down at the Hatteras East Scarp, right at the Wall. Many old engineers live there, so I'd be with my own kind, and they've got a little tourist funicular that carries you up to a Wall-top restaurant where you can have breakfast on the terrace and look out over the ocean and see the morning sun light up the Wall for miles in each direction.

That would suit me just fine.

I got a shock talking to Gleason this afternoon.

I'd been complaining to him about my case, saying the whole

thing had been trumped up in order to silence me so I couldn't expose the dangerous situation at the Wall, and that I realized I'd undoubtedly lose and be forced into retirement.

He began looking uncomfortable and cleared his throat several times, and finally he said he didn't think retirement was too likely a possibility for me.

"Why not?" I asked.

"That's an administrative matter, and the Security Court doesn't handle that category."

"I know, but won't the court refer me to a disciplinary board for the proper action?"

"I'm afraid not. If the magistrate had dismissed the charges, the prosecutor would have turned the matter over to the disciplinary board in this district, but in view of your arraignment, the judicial context of the case has passed to a higher level, beyond mere discipline."

"That damned Army lawyer never told me that!"

"He may have assumed you knew—but you'll be interested to know that we are mounting a campaign to modify the severity of the existing—"

"Just a minute. Are you saying that if I'm found guilty, the Security Court can do just one thing?"

"Ah, yes. In essence, yes. This is what we're trying to change. Not that precisely, but the question of duration. We feel—we strongly feel—that common humanity requires a probationary period, so that after two or three years, a case can be reconsidered for possible readmission, which is not contemplated under the present . . ."

I won't transcribe any more. What it means is that if I am found guilty, I won't be disciplined, they won't even lock me up for a while, the way they used to do with common criminals back when they had prisons.

They don't lock you up any more. They lock you out.

Exclusion.

You can never get back in.

AUGUST 21

I am sleeping badly despite the EZ dosage and the comforter, and once in a while I have a seizure of anger that makes me pace around the cell, makes me yell and curse at that little bug-eyedmurid who watches me every minute of the day and all through the night.

AUGUST 22

I am forcing myself to keep under control. Yesterday my murid started buzzing, and a doctor in a white jacket came and looked at me and asked me some questions—I guess they were upset because I smashed my Vidipix—and luckily I was able to give him the right answers, so he went away, and nothing happened, but if I'm not careful, they may decide to put me in the maximum security section. And I have other plans.

Trying to analyze what I feel. This rage. When I have to yell, I get inside the comforter. It is soundproof. I think about Northeast, but except for Dr. Matthews I have never seen those people, nor they me; they are voices on the telemin and ciphers on the screen. They are nobody. Most of the time I run the Librex, reading at random: botany, zoology, etc. How plants talk. How trees migrate. The sex life of reptiles.

Northeast didn't do a thing to me; I can't be angry at those zeroes. You might say Dr. Matthews had no personal animus toward me, he behaved quite properly and normally; given his manifest stupidity, what else could he have done? After having reported me to DIPS—I am convinced he did that—he let matters take their course and was indifferent to my fate. Why should he bother to make the ten-minute glassway trip from Boston to inform the court of my commendations? One regional director is as good as another. It is the systems that count. The trees are interdependent, they rely on one another for defense against disease and insect attack, and they apparently take collective decisions to move when conditions start to get bad for them—Dr. Braaten jots that they generate their best seeds on the side that is in the desired migration direction—but we are not interdependent any more. We have moved up the scale from family to tribe to nation to what we have now, which is not really a nation any longer, although the forms are maintained, like the habit of saying "we." We are not really we. We are you and me, we are ones—singles. We are separate beings, independent.

AUGUST 23

Made an experiment today. Every other weekday afternoon we get to go to the workshop for a couple of hours of arts and crafts. Today the felid let me operate the neural art frame, which contains a hologen for air-painting. Using a mirror, I created my own full-length 3-D portrait and noted down the settings. Then I removed the hologen from the frame and air-painted its image in the empty space. I don't think anybody else uses the frame. It could be weeks before they find out. I tucked the hologen under my shirt—it is the size of a flute—and returned to my cell. In the last few minutes of dusk before the evening lights go on, I reproduced my portrait right in front of me—between me and the murid—and slipped off to one side. Sure enough, the murid continued to watch my image, not me, and once I was satisfied of that, I erased it.

   This will be useful.

The exercise yard is seldom used, and no wonder. It is a walled rectangle the size of a basketball court, paved with asphalt that gets sticky in the heat. The air is as heavy as sweat, and when there's a breeze, sand comes sifting in off the top of the wall. There is nothing much to do there except jog around or play handball. My murid (he goes with me everywhere) stands in the middle watching me.

   The wall is about three meters high. On the north side the stones are out of line. The ground must have settled there.

If you get too close to the wall, the murid starts to hum. If you don't back off then, the hum becomes a buzz, summoning an ursid.

For the past week I have been working out for two-hour stretches in the late afternoon. That is the maximum time allowed. They must think I'm crazy, trotting around in the summer heat, bouncing that handball off the wall.

There is no guard on the roof of the center, as far as I can tell. They rely on the murid.

Dr. Grandgent told me that if the Wall goes, it will go fast. The *tregadyne rip*, he called it. The first jet through a breach would shoot twenty kilometers inland, taking the crest off the Rampart the way you might scoop whipped cream off your sundae. And that would just be the beginning.

AUGUST 28

Every day is like every other day. I try not to think too much about the Wall, which is leaking, getting ready for the tregadyne rip. The systems don't know, but the trees do. They must be starting to migrate. I doubt they will have time. I keep the hologen under the mattress. Its settings are in my mind. The calluses on my hands are thick now. In the exercise yard I do knee-bends and handstands while my murid watches. Every day is like every other day, but tomorrow will be different.

AUGUST 29

Out!

SEPTEMBER 4

On the Wall at last. Last night a storm almost blew me off—spray and driving rain and gusts of wind. Now the heat of day has dried me. My hair and beard are stiff with salt.

SEPTEMBER 5

I've found a temporary refuge inside the east tower of the Hudson impact-energy complex.

SEPTEMBER 6

The intake rams boom and sigh like giant mollusks opening and closing their valves, heartbeats of the sea. I can feel the vibrations through these tons of superstructure towering high over the Atlantic.

I'm safe here for now. The control room overhead is staffed by fixed felids—I climbed up for a quick look—but I can't rule out the possibility that there is a patrol ursid somewhere.

My clothes are rags, my boots are wrecked. I must have slept twenty hours up here.

I feel rested, but I am hungry, and thirst is bothering me a lot. When darkness comes, I'll have to move on.

My escape from the detention center went just as I'd planned it. As soon as I entered the exercise yard, I painted my air-image with the hologen and made sure the murid was fixed on it. Then I went to the north wall, where the uneven settling of the stones provided a few rudimentary holds, clawed my way up and over. The drop on the other side was a couple of meters deeper, into a ditch, but the ground was cushioned by drifts of blown sand.

I knew I had two hours before the murid would give the signal. I like to think of the damned thing trying to get the image to move, humming at it and then buzzing, and the ursid trotting out to grab a nonexistent arm and hauling off a mittful of air, coming back to try again, and finally the felid-in-charge would have to come out to see what the trouble was.

They probably would have assumed that I would head across the Bay Valley to Plymouth or Boston.

I went south instead.

By dark—when the search would have begun in earnest—I was climbing the Barnstable Slope.

Walked all night.

By dawn I was at the edge of the Nantucket Waste, about eight kilometers northeast of the Chappaquiddick Rise. I dug a hole in the sand and roofed it with driftwood, scattered sand on top, and crawled in to wait out the day. Had a terrible thirst.

The Nantucket Waste is a tract about eighty kilometers square, officially under reclamation and development; in fact, nothing has been done, as the soil is poor and the minerals not worth bothering about. I'd seen it only from the air. From there it looks like an ordinary uninhabited plain: no trees, just a freckling of low vegetation; not a single building, no roads, nothing. An occasional survey party must go through—I saw old wheel-tracks in several places—but I can't imagine that anyone has ever crossed it the way I did, by foot. It took me three days—three nights, I should say, as by day I had to burrow and hide from the hovers.

The Waste is a stinking salt desert and a monument to pre-Wall industrial civilization. Decade after decade, every city along the old seaboard poured its filth into the rivers and bays, or hauled it out by barge and dumped it into the ocean, and this evil sludge is lying in clumps and heaps and hillocks all around me, festering in the blazing heat of day, together with the skeletons of sunken boats and tangles of nets and drag-lines and the bones of fish and birds. Mounds of ancient industrial garbage; piles of rusted junk, old refrigerators and crumpled car bodies; acid spills spread like rainbows in the sand; dead rivers of dried and crusty tar; exploded oil drums, chunks of concrete; strips and shreds of plastic that lift in the breeze and dance like ghosts across the plain.

In the starlight of the second night I walked through a puddle of acid which burned holes in my boots. I had to patch them by stuffing weeds inside.

Even in the tracts that are clear of junk, the Waste is foul. Pools of brine lie in the low places. Some are solid pans of salt. It smells of death and hopelessness. The shrubs and weeds that grow here have a deformed look and provide shelter for snakes. There are few birds of any kind, and most are flesh-eaters: hawks, gulls, owls, vultures. I saw gophers and rats; sometimes I would catch a glimpse of a fox, and once in the distance I saw several four-legged creatures bigger than foxes, which I feared might be wild dogs, but maybe they were foxes magnified by the heat haze.

I'd been able to bring just a pocketful of energy crackers with me, and these soon gave out, but it wasn't hunger that almost killed me, it was thirst. I licked dew from the stones, but it tasted salty, and so did the rainwater caught in the hollows of the rocks. My lips swelled; my tongue got big. I was seeing mirages—a city of silver towers, a parade of giant ursids, the Wall. Only the Wall was real, but it was far away to the south, and it kept changing in the heat; sometimes it reared up in the sky so close I could almost touch it, and then it would shrink down to the edge of the horizon, no thicker than a ribbon—a double ribbon, with the lesser rise of the Rampart in front of it. I remember running toward it, staggering and yelling, falling down in a dead sleep of exhaustion, and waking in terror and pain to find a crab biting my leg. I flung the crab off, then scrambled after it, grabbed it and broke it apart with my hands right in front of a vulture which had landed and was watching me maybe a dozen paces away. I think it was a real vulture. I had black spots before my eyes and a steel drum beating in my head, and the vulture might have been a fantasy air-painted by my thirst.

I would have died out in the Nantucket Waste if I hadn't come across the museum.

It was near dawn when I noticed something rising out of the plain far away. At first it seemed to be a giant cleaver-shaped rock, tilted up at an angle. As I drew closer and the sky began to lighten, it took on the form of a man-made thing, like a strange slanted tower, maybe the remains of an old oil-drilling operation; then I saw what it really was: the prow of a huge ship, thrust up out of the sand and the salty muck—a lonely and mysterious survival of centuries past, like the half-buried temple of some ancient religion.

I hurried toward it, drawn by curiosity and my fear of day-light—soon I would have to seek cover from the hover patrols—and by my terrible thirst—perhaps I would find a puddle of uncontaminated rainwater somewhere around that monstrous prow. Now I could see other shapes around it, other vessels, all small by comparison: a smashed fishing smack, a motor launch, half of what might have been a trawler, a couple of cabin cruisers, all wrecked and rusted there in the shadow of that enormous ship.

As I approached, I could discern signs of past human en-deavor—cracked patches of what had once been a paved road, the tangled ruins of a wire fence, a shed with a window in it and a little sign nailed beneath that read TICKETS. This was all that remained of some promoter's dream...an exhibition of ship-wrecks. He must have hauled the smaller boats from wherever they had foundered and clustered them around his main attrac-tion. I picked my way among the hulks. Gulls flapped up from their roosts, screaming at me. Something like an owl stared at me through a porthole of the giant ship. Along the upthrust prow above me was a name in letters scarred by centuries of weathering: ANDREA DORIA.

The sun was up. There were two vultures high in the sky—except one was a hover. I could hear the high whistling sigh of its MOG gyros. I ducked inside the museum entrance, a door cut in the side of the big ship. It was dark and damp in there. I was somewhere in the hold. Felt my way toward threads of light that came from above, caught hold of a railing and pulled myself into another compartment; worked my way up—or rather sort of sideways, as the ship was tilted up at such an angle—into a larger section that might have been crew's quar-ters. I could see fish skeletons scattered in the corners, bird bones, old nests crusted with guano, feathers, shreds of rotted cloth, buttons.

I kept going, climbing corridors using cabin doorways for handholds, spreadeagled my way across the floor of a dining room—the heap of junk at the lower end might have been chairs and tables once—and into what turned out to be a lounge. There were wooden steps there, a sort of ladder. The museum proprietor must have had it installed for his customers—the only surviving fragment of his enterprise, apart from the ticket shed and the fence. I mounted to the bar and stopped short in alarm, face to face with a dead youth, hardly more than a boy, who leaned upright behind the counter staring at me with wide horrible unseeing eyes—but then I saw what it really was: another abandoned relic—a murid, dressed in a barman's jacket and bowtie, its facial housing covered by a painted mask and topped by a wig. It was ghastly—the mask was lumpy and discolored, and the jacket streaked with gull droppings—but at least the thing was not human. I exclaimed in relief and disgust—said something, laughed, I don't remember—and to my amazement the creature spoke, its sound track shrill and abrasive. *"May I take your drink order, sir or madam?"* My voice must have activated its vocal servomotor. *"May I take your drink order . . . ?"* It seemed to lean toward me, miming a bartender's confidential encouragement, and it smiled, splitting the rotting mask—I could see the sheen of metal where the painted lips tore apart. One arm moved, as though reaching for a glass underneath the counter. I shivered with revulsion, broke into a sweat. Something small—a rat?— scuttled out from some hiding place and went thumping down the ladder and away. I backed down the first few steps, staring at the hideous boy's mask that leaned grinning at me, then I turned and clattered the rest of the way down. A gull perched in a porthole flapped off outside, screaming. *"May I take your drink order . . . ?"* I went scrambling through the tilted dining room, with that croaking voice echoing in my ears. It may have been my imagination, but throughout the day I thought I heard it now and then, rustily repeating its hospitable invitation to noisy gulls and visiting rats.

I explored the ship, avoiding the part that lay buried in what had been the ocean floor, fearing the darkness. If I fell there—! I dug out a few small treasures: a hammer, a coil of plastic cable, several rusty marlin spikes. In a pile of rubbish at the bottom of a corridor I found some cans of various sizes and opened them with the hammer and a spike. Most were spoiled, some exploded at the first punch of the spike—I was drenched with wads of stinking stuff—but I did find a few that had survived: peeled tomatoes swimming in their juice, anchovies, artichoke hearts, meat extract, and some small bottles of reddish liquid slightly bitter to the taste.

I slept on the boat deck, wedged in a corner in the shade of one slanting funnel, slept as the sun crossed the sky and sank, slept beneath the stars that glittered above that ghostly wasteland, slept and dreamed of Julia, of freedom, of death.

Sometime after midnight I worked my way out of the ship.

By daylight I had reached the Rampart, which is treeless and empty here, no more than a mass of rock rearing out of the dunes of sand. I climbed it, crossed it, descended.

I was at the Wall.

SEPTEMBER 8

I had no intention of climbing the Wall. My idea was to walk along the embankment, following it southwest, checking for seepage as I went—but when I got there and stood in its morning shadow looking up at it, something broke within me, a kind of joy and defiance, and I knew I had to go up, patrols or no patrols, and walk the Wall. (Halfway up I regretted that impulse, but it was too late then.) With my spikes and cable, I was able to hammer and haul my way over the bad spots, but I was weak, and clouds of gnats swarmed in my eyes and invaded my nostrils; when I reached the top I was so spent I just lay helpless in the sun. Slept. Woke to the sound of a hover approaching. I was trapped, no escape. What I did—it was my only chance—was to use the hologen to air-paint a 3-D image of Wall-top stone over me. The hover scan is a visual one. The craft accepted the false image and passed directly above me without slowing or circling and went on its way.

I was afraid the hologen would be useless against patrol ursids, however. To avoid them, I would have to get off the top of the Wall, out of their track sights, which meant swinging over the side on my cable, secured to my spikes. In the two days it took me to reach the Hudson complex, I had to do this stunt twice—the same ursid, first going north, then coming south on its return—and of course I couldn't sleep, dangling over the embankment that way, nor could I risk sleeping on the Wall either, and this, together with the big storm that almost blew me over that night, reduced me to a desperate wreck by the time I reached the Hudson towers on the afternoon of September 5, six days after my escape from Atlantis North.

Walking the Wall—there is nothing like it, it makes you feel like a god, you are on a granite tightrope between two worlds, land and water, the great mass of ocean sliding up at you beating and frothing, and on the other side, the earth rolling away low and far as if shrinking from the threat of the sea, and you are walking on the very knife-edge of this torment, this tension which knots and churns beneath your feet, this war of elements, like good and evil (but which is good? which is evil?), but no, I am putting it badly, the Wall is not to be understood that way, it is not reason but feeling, it is pure, it stands outside morality, something men built which transcends human values.

It has taken me nearly three days to reach Baltimore Canyon, my old territory. At this moment I stand at the point where the rungs lead down. Here Julia followed me; here I fought the ursid. It seems long ago, not just a few weeks.

On the way I kept watching for seepage, saw plenty of water in the trench, but from this height I couldn't be sure it wasn't just rain runoff. At several points the water had overflowed the embankment and was spreading into the flatlands. Then—it was near noon today—it began to recede. The level sank rapidly, and it was gone; the trench was empty. The pumps had gone into operation again. I knew that within a few hours the seepage would start surfacing once more, but the thought struck me, I don't know how, but it had never occurred to me before—that is, was it possible that what I have taken to be seepage is simply the residue of an invasion that has already been sealed by the Deeps? That it will continue to well up for a while and then disappear—?

No, I don't think that.

It is seepage. Fresh seepage. And it is getting worse.

SEPTEMBER 10

In Baltimore.

Hiding out in the jungle north of the old railroad station. The excluded colony is nearby, maybe two hundred meters southeast. I can't see them and don't want to, but I can smell what they're cooking—roast pig, if I had to guess. I can hear them gabbling and shouting. They are like animals. I wouldn't mind a slice of pork, but I doubt if I could eat in their presence, from sheer disgust.

Night before last I climbed down the Wall where the old rungs are, walked across the flatlands, and ascended the Rampart. I broke into a couple of abandoned houses, searching for food, found not so much as a crumb. It has been years since anyone lived up there. I came across a thicket of blackberry bushes, ate a lot of berries. From the ridge I could see the lights of Neptune down in the Valley. One string of them marked my street— Gorton Avenue—and about midway would be my house. My former house. The word "home" occurred to me, I don't know why. You don't hear it very often. It is a mere survival from the past, and of course people don't use it in the old sense, just as they will say they are natives of such-and-such a place, even though it is meaningless. We all come from identical Generation

Centers—there are four of them (mine was the one in Pitts-burgh)—and spend our foetushoods and baby years in lifecamps operated by the central grid system of the Department of Health, Education and Welfare. We are natives of nowhere.

I waited out the day on the Rampart ridge, dozing in the bushes, between bouts of diarrhea from those blackberries.

At dusk I started down the slope.

The moon was up. The air was still and warm. I worked my way through the ranks of pines and cedars that form a belt along the lower edge of the Rampart and crossed the rough-cut fire lane to where the Neptune parkland begins. The trees and shrubs here are trimmed and tended by a pair of Class D murids which are not tracked to react to human presence. I walked right past the shed where they stand at night to keep out of the damp.

A stream runs through the middle of the park. I headed for it to slake the thirst which has plagued me ever since I left the detention center, savoring in anticipation the pure sweet water I would gulp down. I kneeled beside the stream, plunged my hands in, bathed my face, then cupped my palms and raised them for a drink. The water was briny. Tasted of salt. I spat it out and moved to a different place to try again, but it was the same. That stream was saline. Not a little, a lot. I crouched there, my mouth and tongue stinging from the salt, amazed. It was even worse than I had thought. What I had tasted was the Atlantic. A filament of ocean had worked through the hy-droperm, through the Deeps, through the Rampart flexogen seal, and into the Valley itself. Who could tell how far it went and how widespread it was?

The parkland was silent in the moonlight. The gardener-murids stood like rakes in their shed. I had the sensation that the ground was soggy and yielding under my feet, that at any moment vast hunks of it would cave in and vanish, the trees sucked down into a subterranean gulf, with salty geysers shooting up under the building force of the driving waters—that the Rampart would start to rip and slide, leaving the Wall standing as an isolated and useless pathway of stone in the middle of a vast upwelling of the sea.

Not that, not yet. There is still time—days or weeks, maybe months—time to save what could be moved inland, time to save the people, but I am certain that up in Northeast control headquarters the screens show that all is well, nothing amiss on the flashboards. What could I do that I had not already done? Could I run through the streets of Neptune shouting out an alarm, yelling like the madman maybe I am by now? The town ursids would grab me within five minutes, and everybody would go back to sleep.

I waded the stream and went to the edge of the parkland, crouched by the roadside in the shadows of the last trees, a community of birches which I could imagine struggling to carry out a group decision to migrate with all possible speed, one agonizingly slow generational step at a time, lofting their seed across the road, which seed in turn, when germinated and sprouted and grown, would scatter its offspring farther west, so that the elderly birches left behind, sickening in the salty soil, might hope that some of their descendants would survive in the slow-motion march to inland safety. The tribe would not die.

And what about me? Was I prepared to sacrifice myself for my tribe? I couldn't help smiling at this, it was so ridiculous.

It is the Wall I want to save.

In the middle of the night—I am still referring to last night—I crossed the parkside road and entered Neptune, keeping in the shadows as much as possible. Most houses were dark. In a few I could detect the dim glow of the stimulators, heard an occasional moan of joy.

I entered my old place silently, having removed my boots. All was still. In the gloom of the living room I could make out the dark rectangles of Hilda's neural art and the glassy Vidipix screen covering the far wall. I went straight to the kitchen for my first decent meal in many days. As I stood there stuffing myself, I became aware in that closed space of my odor, so powerful I feared it might actually wake Hilda. As soon as my hunger was appeased, I stripped and showered, dried myself, and padded naked to my old room to see if by chance some of my clothes still hung in the closet. Maybe Hilda hadn't cleared them out yet.

I stopped in the doorway. My bed was empty, but the room wasn't. Someone was in the stimulator. I could see the figure inside the electroexcitor envelope; the machine was humming vigorously. I tiptoed closer. Who was it—Hilda? She had her own stimulator, but it might be broken. I stared down at the ecstatic face. Recognized Bloom. That little bastard had taken my job, my room, even my stimulator!

As a precaution against an untimely awakening, I adjusted the controls of the stimulator, advancing the timer as far as it would go and tuning up the rippler, the pulser, etc., taking, I must confess, a perverse satisfaction in the thought of Bloom after such a strenuous night. He would be a mere rag for days.

My clothes had been removed from the closet. Bloom's were in their place, and, unfortunately, we are of quite different sizes, as he is short and skinny. What I'd worn in prison were putrid shreds, though, and I had no choice. I wedged myself into one of Bloom's coveralls, leaving it unzipped to the navel so I wouldn't split it open, and took a pair of his rubberized sandals, which did, to some extent, stretch. I packed up some food, fed my old clothes and boots into the mulcher, and left the house.

My duty machine was in the garage—Bloom's machine now, I supposed. I pushed it out to the street, to avoid making noise, then started it, and headed for Baltimore. I took the old Valley highway instead of cutting north to pick up the glassway, where I knew there would be patrols. My object was to get to Dr. Grandgent and insist that he intervene directly in this emergency. With his prestige and contacts, he would be able to get through to important people like Dragomine or one of the White House scientific advisers, maybe a senator or congressman—at least I hoped so, but I didn't know if he'd have the guts to do it, and I wasn't sure whether anyone would listen to an old man so long out of touch with the world, and whose name by now might mean nothing.

The old highway was built as a construction road and has been little used since the glassway was finished some fifty years ago. It is poorly maintained, full of potholes, ragged at the edges. The only traffic is local—trucks from the farms and the occasional wheeled murid messenger. By day the countryside has a prosperous and fruitful look with its fields and orchards and greenhouses, cattle grazing and pigs and turkeys in their runs and farmer-robots bumping along on tractors, but at night it is deserted and deathly still. I crossed the entire Valley without meeting a single vehicle or seeing a living soul. The damp of evening seemed to bring out old marine odors, giving an acid tang to the air. Fog drifted across the fields, hiding the barns and the greenhouses, swallowing the woods.

It was full daylight when I reached the old shoreline and drove up the Delaware Slope, heading northwest for Dover. There is no bypass. I had to go through the town—a village, really, in terms of inhabitants. Half-empty, buildings boarded up, whole blocks without a sign of life. Population control and the westward migration have left hundreds of places like this: crumbling remnants of what were once vigorous and productive urban centers, ghost towns gone to wilderness, streets torn apart by weeds and rain-wash, heaps of rusted vehicles and other junk in vacant lots among burnt-out building shells. I saw more rats than people in Dover.

North of the town, I decided to take the glassway to cross the Chesapeake Flats, otherwise it would have taken me hours on the little country roads, which might be impassable in places. There was plenty of glassway traffic, which made me feel less conspicuous, but I went into a cold sweat passing the ursid station at Sparrow's Point—fatigue and nerves catching up with me— and took the first ramp down after that. I kept checking the rear scan for patrol cars, but on the back roads I followed through the outskirts of Baltimore there was virtually no traffic in either direction, and no wonder; the pavement was riddled with pits in the good stretches, and elsewhere little more than a memory. A couple of times I had to stop and get out to hack down vines so the machine could squeeze through.

In north Baltimore I stopped at a track robot control station to ask directions to Johns Hopkins, but the operator had never heard of such a place and began showing a curiosity about me I didn't care for. I must have looked strange, with my bulk crammed into a small man's coverall and my windburnt face and calloused hands. He may have suspected I was an excluded wandering about outside my colony area. I broke off and left, hoping he wouldn't notify the police.

As soon as I reached a place I recognized as being fairly close to Dr. Grandgent's—the old railroad station—I worked the machine into a thicket until it was hidden from sight. Then I pushed my way deeper into the weeds and vines and settled down to wait.

SEPTEMBER 12

I didn't wait long. I was too nervous and impatient. Besides, I realized that here in the city it would be safer to move by day. There are no streetlights in Baltimore except around the air terminal and the packing plants. I might lose my way in the darkness or sprain an ankle stumbling over something. Beyond that, the proximity of the excluded colony worried me. Those creatures probably prowl about scavenging at night and would be capable of doing me harm—they wouldn't recognize me as a free citizen (they don't dare approach us; on the contrary, they hide), but might mistake me as being one of themselves, i.e., legitimate prey.

As I walked along the ruined streets, I had the feeling they were watching me, following me. I heard rustlings in the high weeds and bird calls that didn't sound quite like bird calls. I picked up a rusty iron bar with a spike on one end, part of an old fence, to use in case I was attacked.

The midday sun beat down hard. I was lathering like a horse inside Bloom's skintight coveralls. Flies and gnats and bees darted through the air. Once in a while a commercial hover droned across the sky.

It took me an hour to reach Dr. Grandgent's tumbledown old mansion.

I climbed the porch steps, taking care to avoid the splits in the boards. Knocked on the door. No answer. I waited, knocked again, louder, and called his name. Nothing. I went inside, keeping an eye out for his felid. I didn't want the damned thing jumping out at me. "Dr. Grandgent...? Dr. Grandgent...?" There was absolute silence.

I was puzzled. The old man never left the house, as far as I knew. Was he asleep while the felid was out shopping? I looked in the study, the dining room, the bedrooms in back, all empty. Upstairs I checked room after room, opening rotting doors to peer into dust and cobwebs. I even climbed to the attic, where a tree had thrust a branch through the window, and bird nests clung to the rafters.

I returned downstairs for another look, being worried now. Dr. Grandgent was gone. His things were still in the house— stacks of books and papers on his desk in the study, and his suits in the bedroom closet—but he wasn't.

The only room I hadn't seen was the kitchen.

The felid—"Professor McKay"—had kept it clean and tidy, but it wasn't tidy now. The table was overturned, the chair broken, crockery and pans were scattered all over, the window was smashed. It looked as if some terrific battle had taken place there. Had the felid jumped its track, gone wild, and torn everything apart—even assaulted Dr. Grandgent? Such things are extremely rare, but do happen, and I knew that this felid had certain little defects (the old man wouldn't have bothered sending it off for the necessary periodic overhauls).

Then I saw it—part of it—lying under the table. What I'd taken at first to be a mop handle was a leg. The creature was in pieces. One of its grips, wrenched off, was among the crockery, its dented torso was in the doorway of the pantry closet, and the head—I went to the broken window—was outside in a rosebush.

Only an ursid was strong enough to do that.

Dr. Grandgent's felid, loyal to the end, had fought to defend its master.

And Dr. Grandgent was missing.

I hurried out to the porch, gripping my iron bar. I knew I had to get back to my machine ... to go where, I had no clear idea.

As I started down the steps, they rose up out of the tangle of wild growth at the edge of the yard: three burly DIPS agents in their gray uniforms and square caps, and a pair of stocky police ursids.

I didn't hesitate. I ran down the steps, heading for the gate. One of the ursids moved to block me. I slammed him on the snout with the bar, bowling him over, and burst out to the street. I could hear the steps of the second ursid thudding behind me.

A fourth DIPS agent stood there facing me, an agent slighter than the others, holding something pointed at me. A hypogun. It flashed and I felt its bite. Just before I lost consciousness, I saw her face, strangely contorted, almost unrecognizable; but I knew who it was.

PART
THREE

SEPTEMBER 15

My recollections of the last few days are confused. What happened before she shot me—that part is clear. After that . . . well, I was drugged for a while, and then a feeling of hopelessness came over me; I wanted to die and be forgotten, I was swept by shame and despair, thinking about what had become of me.

When I was brought before the court—I was taken back to Atlantis North, which had jurisdiction of my case—I stood there trembling and sniveling like a coward, abasing myself; couldn't help it; I was frightened. A gulf had opened at my feet, and I was about to plunge into it, and nothing could be done to save me. On the contrary, these smug bastards were giving me the final shove, and my whimpering and moaning was music to their ears. You could tell they expected it and approved of it and were gratified by the spectacle. When I realized this, something hardened in me, something fierce and angry came breaking up through my fear, some terrible survival of human viciousness which generations of selective genetic breeding hadn't been able to wipe out. I'm ashamed to admit it now, but I have nothing to lose, so I might as well be honest about it. I asked the colonel if I could whisper something to him—something private and personal—so with that haughty smirk on his stupid face, he leaned toward me over the bench, looking down. I broke his nose with the side of my hand. I could feel the cartilage crack, saw the blood gush as he toppled off to one side, astonished.

I don't remember much after that except considerable pain. I suppose the ursid grabbed me and tore at me for a while. My right shoulder has bruise marks that seem to go to the bone, and my left leg is numb from the knee down. I haven't access to a mirror, but I must look mashed up. I can feel lumps and swellings all over my face, and a lower incisor is missing.

At some point when I was in what I suppose was the detention center infirmary—I was wrapped in bandages and strapped to a bed—I was visited by the lawyer, Hooper Gleason, who came to give me formal notification that my assault on the judge had ruled out any possibility of appeal. His manner had changed. I got the impression that he could hardly bear to be in the same room with me. Granted, I must have been a pitiful and ludicrous sight stretched out there all battered and bandaged, but that shouldn't have evoked repugnance—the same repugnance I'd seen on the face of the doctor who had stopped by a few minutes earlier to take a look at me. For a moment I couldn't understand it, and then I had a flash of recognition, for their expressions—Gleason's and the doctor's—had mirrored what I myself had felt on those few occasions when I had happened to glimpse one of those creatures whom we are taught from birth to regard with disgust.

It was then that I realized for the first time what I was—what they had made of me. It wasn't the court order (which I could vaguely remember having heard), it wasn't the brutal beating the ursid had given me; it was that look of abhorrence on Gleason's face. I wouldn't have cared if he'd begun upbraiding me for my stupidity or abused me for having wasted his time, or even taunted me with sarcastic predictions about the torments and degradations that awaited me—no, that would have been a relief in a way, it would have been treating me as a fellow human, someone with whom he still had some points of contact.

* * *

I've been trying to reconstruct those last moments outside Dr. Grandgent's house in Baltimore. I remember her face, Julia's face, and I remember how she looked—a strange expression, tense and strained. But what was she feeling then? Was it anger, was it triumph? Was it something else? I relive that scene over and over again, trying to puzzle it out, seeing it all in my mind. I had knocked down the first ursid and dashed through the privet to the street, where she was. I could hear the second ursid just behind me. She would have seen that clearly. She was facing me. She would have realized I couldn't get away. Police ursids are fast. They can cover one hundred meters in just above seven seconds. Nothing on two legs can outrun them, except maybe an ostrich. So she didn't need to use the hypogun. In another second the ursid would have grabbed me. She would have known that. So she must have shot me, not out of duty, but to save me from the grab.

If that is true—and I can think of no other explanation for what she did—then she did it to spare me pain, and that expression on her face, it must have been one not of anger but of anguish.

But if she saw me now—? Wouldn't she look at me the way Gleason looked at me, the way the doctor looked at me? With that same aversion?

SEPTEMBER 16

I managed to save the micropen by concealing it in the only hiding place available to a man who is about to be stripped, shaved, and shorn. Luckily it is a small model.

SEPTEMBER 20

This is my third day in this place.

At first I thought it was some kind of processing center.

Now I know what it is: an excluded colony. It is fenced and

guarded. There is no way out. I am a prisoner among prisoners, a piece of human trash swept into a corner to age and die.

On the morning of the 17th, a pair of police ursids bundled me into a car and took the glassway into Boston—I got a glimpse of the Northeast headquarters building and could imagine Dr. Matthews in his corner office smugly reading the misinformation on his screens—and then a few miles north through some sleazy suburbs. The area was ravaged by fire a few years ago, and whole blocks were burned, but it wasn't worth rebuilding. The population was leaving anyhow. It remains as it was, a charred wasteland with a scattering of buildings here and there.

We didn't go far. We passed a checkpoint at a gate and were waved through, entering an enclosed area—a sort of compound with several barracks around the edge of a grassy open space, which had a few sickly trees in it.

We stopped. The ursids made me get out, and then they drove off, leaving me there.

There were some fifteen or twenty people in the open area: men, women, children. I stood there for a while, expecting somebody to come up and tell me what to do and where to go, but nobody approached me except for one of the children, until an adult called it back.

I stood under one of the scraggly trees, watching the people. Some were looking at me, and they seemed to be talking about me. A couple of them laughed and nudged each other, which made me uneasy. What bothered me the most was the sight of the children running around playing. I'd never seen children turned loosed that way; in fact, I'd never seen them at all, except an occasional group being escorted somewhere under supervision. It was different here. Everything was different. I knew that at once, but I couldn't admit it. I was trying to convince myself that this was just a way station, a temporary stopping place. I didn't belong there. I had to believe that. I even told myself that these people couldn't be excluded, that maybe they were in some other category.

But there were the children, running loose. This was such a departure from the norms of social life that I couldn't accept it, I couldn't allow myself to realize what it must mean, and I remember turning my head in other directions, looking at the ground, at the sky, anywhere to keep from seeing those children.

No one came up to me. Nothing happened. The morning crept by. The children played; people came and went. I saw couples. Touching—holding hands, even embracing. The sight gave me contrary sensations of repulsion and curiosity. The person closest to me was an elderly man in a rumpled suit who sat on a wooden bench some twenty paces away. I caught him three or four times casting sly glances at me, but he didn't try to approach me, and finally he got up and walked across the park to one of the barracks.

The sky was clouding, and the wind turned cool. I wore only the rough shirt and trousers which had been issued to me at the infirmary. I began to wonder what I would do for shelter. A distant bell clanged, and I was aware of the odor of food from one of the buildings. It was time for the noon meal. Like little animals, the children dashed whooping off to eat, the adults following them. One of the men beckoned to me. Was I supposed to eat with them? I was hungry, but the idea of sitting among them disturbed me. I didn't want to mingle with them. I had to stay apart. I was different. I *had* to be different.

I stayed out there alone, and it began to rain, a cold soaking rain that soon wet me through, and I stood there discomfited and humiliated, as the water ran down my shaved head and bruised, pulpy face.

Looking for shelter, I went toward one of the barracks, but when I realized there were excluded inside (I saw faces at the windows peering out at me), I tried another building. There were people there, too. One of them opened the main door and waved to me, urging me to come in, but I turned away.

I finally found a toolshed in the back and crept in among the rakes and sickles and spiderwebs. It was there I spent the rest of the day and the night, huddled damp and shivering on the wooden boards, watching the rain drip through the seams in the roofing, and I reflected with bitter satisfaction that when the Atlantic breaks through—tomorrow, next month, next year—the force of the rip will scour all this away like sand. I could see in my mind giant sea jets smashing and raging, splintering everything in their path and scattering the pieces far and wide.

During the night someone opened the door of the shed, and a light flashed across my face, waking me. I tensed myself, ready to ward off an attack, but then the light vanished, the door swung shut again, and my visitor was gone. To defend myself I picked up a rake, prepared to lash out, but no one else came, and I slept fitfully until dawn. In the first light I saw what I had been unable to see before—a dish of food had been left for me, some sort of hash with potatoes and beans in it. I was fiercely hungry but left it where it was. To eat would have been to participate—to admit that I was one of them—an act of surrender.

I crawled outside, stiff and shaky. My clothes were still damp. The day was clear but cold, with frost in the shadows of the barracks. The pale early sun gave no warmth. To ease my thirst I licked dew from the leaves of the trees. The colony was still asleep. I could hear scattered brassy snores. A child began crying—and was silenced with a slap. I went trudging through the wet grass, exploring the confines of the camp. On the west side, where there had once been a road, ran a ditch three meters deep, its far side rimmed by a high barbed-wire fence. I walked parallel to the ditch, heading north. That side, too, was blocked by the fence, with a gate in the middle, behind which was posted an ursid guard, who at once picked up my image and gave me a menacing stare. The eastern boundary likewise was fenced and ditched. The south side was apparently open and unguarded, but the presence of pairs of low pipes protruding from the ground at intervals led me to suspect the existence of an electrovallum, which theory I tested by trying to toss handfuls of gravel across the seemingly innocuous space. Each time there was a crackling sound and tiny ripples of smoke in the air. The gravel vanished—disintegrated.

Disheartened, I returned to the central open space. By this time people were emerging from the barracks, heading for the building which served as a dining hall. I wondered how they spent their time. There was a vegetable garden near the north section of the fence, but it wasn't large enough to occupy more than a few of them. Perhaps they did handicrafts.

I lay down under the spindly little trees where I had sat the day before and dozed off. Once I woke to see the elderly man in the rumpled suit looking at me from his bench. He seemed about to speak, which I discouraged by turning over on my other side. When I woke the second time, I was surrounded by children— eight or nine ragamuffins in dirty clothes. I sat up alarmed, my stomach growling with hunger. "Say, mister, why don't you come inside?" one of them asked. "Why don't you eat?" They edged closer, some grinning, some looking frightened. It was the largest who had spoken, a boy of about twelve. "What's the matter with you, mister?" he said. "You sick?" I eased myself into a crouch and glared at them without answering. "All the others eat," the boy said. "How come you don't?" I could hear adult voices calling them away. Two or three left, but the others remained. "You deaf, mister?" the boy asked. One of the others, a little girl with pigtails, began giggling. Soon they all were laughing, even the ones who seemed afraid of me. They edged closer. In my exhaustion and weakness, I couldn't be sure how well I could withstand a sudden assault by these creatures. The boy, their spokesman, extended one hand, which held a crust of bread. "Don't you want this, mister?" The taunt made me furious. I roared at them, swinging my arms. They went scrambling back, fleeing in different directions.

That second night I dreamed of the West—a dream that may have been, in part, a hunger hallucination, as I had eaten nothing for forty hours. I closed my eyes: the walls of the shed vanished, and I was lifted into the night air, among the stars; Boston fell away beneath me, and the east whirled beyond the far horizon.

The West of my dreams wasn't the one I'd known on my

vacation trips. It was that, yes, but different. More. I saw once
again the great resorts—the City of Mirrors, Glacierland, the Sky
Sweep, etc.—but what filled my soul was the sum of it, the spirit
of the West, a vastness and beauty that invades your consciousness, that expands your awareness of self so that you achieve an
identity with the harmony and grandeur of nature: the mountains,
plains, deserts, the fields of snow beneath the infinite sky.

What the West offers is solitude. It is amazing how they manage
it. There must be more than thirty million citizens in the West
at any given moment—residents and tourists—and although the
place is vast, you would be bound to run into other people now
and then without the precise controls they have established. I
remember once at Pike's when I was resting at one of the lodges,
I saw a fellow come tramping out of the pines—some screwup
in the tempex—and he stopped short when he saw me, staring
at me in great annoyance, just as I looked angrily his way. When
I got back to Colorado Springs, I registered a strong protest with
the Tourist Board, and probably the other fellow did, too, and
naturally they apologized left and right and immediately made
an investigation, but the damage had been done, and no amount
of apology could restore my inner peace. Incidents of that kind
are rare, though. You can go for days—for weeks—without catching sight of another soul.

Of course, uninterrupted solitude is not to everyone's taste,
and many vacationers frequent the entertainment resorts, of which
there are dozens, and then there are the Attirement Centers and
track-robot Olympics, etc. One interesting spa is the City of Mirrors, where you find yourself in the middle of a crowd of persons,
and each one is you. You see yourself coming and going, side
views, back views, close-ups; for a dedicated narcissist it must be
pure heaven.

There are also historical pageants showing how people lived
in other eras, which I never got around to visiting. My preference
was the Desert Experience, which I did twice. They say this has
been recreated on the telemax, so you can do it at home (if you
are high enough on the social scale to rate a home unit), but I
doubt that technology can successfully imitate the real thing—

the dry limitless sweep of space in which earth and sky seem to
unite, with you in the middle, and you feel you are nothing and
everything at the same time.

Perhaps it was this that drew me to the Wall. It is West-like
in its majesty and emptiness, mountain and desert together, the
most sublime expression of the American Dream.

I woke to frosty air that chilled my bones and hunger that gnawed
my guts. I was too weak to drag myself outside, but I had nowhere
to go, had nothing within me but my determination to remain
apart.

They came for me some time before midday. Two of the men
hauled me out of the shed, and despite my efforts to resist, they
walked me into the communal dining hall and propped me on a
bench at one of the long tables there. Then, under the direction
of the elderly man in the rumpled suit, they tried to force food
into me—spoonfuls of soup, chunks of roast meat. To make me
open my mouth, they pinched my nostrils shut. I spat most of it
out, gagging and choking when some slipped down my throat.
"He's a hard case, all right," I remember the elderly man re-
marking. A crowd gathered to observe this torture. The children
pushed up close. "He smells bad," one of them said. The women
crowded around, too, pushing the children out of the way to get
a better view. I felt suffocated by their nearness, their breaths,
their faces, bodies. Food streaked my filthy clothes. The edge of
a spoon had cut my lip when I jerked my head aside, and there
was blood in my mouth. "Give the man some air," someone
ordered. I shut my eyes. My face was wiped with a cloth. "You'd
better eat," one of them told me. "You'll get sick if you don't."
I kept my eyes shut, refused to reply. At length the efforts to feed
me ceased, and I was dragged to a chair set against a wall and
tied to it with cords around my wrists and ankles. I could hear
them discussing what to do with me. "Let's call the felid," one
man said. Others disagreed. "Not yet. Give him another day or
two. He won't hold out . . ."

It was their dinner hour, and they left me alone while they ate, the whole horde of them—there must have been more than one hundred persons altogether, jammed in at six long tables. The noise and confusion were unspeakable, children mixed in with adults, and people getting up and moving around, passing plates, going back to the kitchen, stopping here and there to speak to others—to yell, I should say, in order to be heard above the din.

It seemed to me that the division of the diners at different tables was not just a matter of convenience; that is, each group seemed to hold itself apart from the others, and I got the impression that there was some underlying hostility between them— certainly there was little, if any, communication among the tables—but perhaps I am wrong, for aside from some differences in such trifling matters as hair and skin color, they all seemed the same to me.

Something happened in the middle of the meal that stunned me, it was so extraordinary.

A young woman entered. As I watched her making her way among the tables, I saw that she had a strange shape in front, pushed out under her dress, as if she were obese—except I could tell she wasn't obese.

Then I remembered an image I'd seen once years ago—a screen from an old medical text I happened to run across on the Librex— and it hit me: she was pregnant. Pregnant!

I was shocked, of course, and tried not to look at her, even though I was unable to tear my eyes away. The astonishing thing was that I was the only one who paid any attention to her. The other people went right on eating and talking, hardly giving her a glance. This bewildered me. What did it mean? Didn't they see her? Didn't they know what was wrong?

I knew they saw her, and I knew they didn't care. It meant nothing to them—and there could be only one explanation: for them it was an ordinary sight, they were used to it, it was the norm around here.

And the realization swept over me that I was in a viviparous community—that all these people (most of them, certainly) had been *born*.

This sank my spirits lower still.

SEPTEMBER 27

Since that day they have kept me in a room on the top floor of one of the barracks. The door is locked day and night. I could get out through the window and slide down the rainpipe, but it would be pointless. I couldn't get past the fence or the electrovallum. At least I am alone, except when one of them comes to bring me food and take away the pot I am forced to use for my sanitary needs.

Once I realized I would be allowed privacy, I decided to eat.

I have refused to speak, however. The elderly man has dropped by every day to talk to me, but I give him no sign of recognition and remain mute. After a while, he leaves.

His name is O'Connor, and I was surprised when he told me his age—fifty-six, the same as mine—for he looks more than twice that old, with his wrinkled face and rheumy eyes. His hands are freckled with liver spots. Beside this fellow, I am a living illustration of the benefits of the Juvenor (even though I am a weak and beaten-down specimen now).

O'Connor doesn't seem to realize that he and the others are the outcasts of a social system that has no use for them. He even seems to feel that they are better off than people in the outside world, about which he knows very little, and most of that incorrect. For example, he told me with scorn that "those folks" were all eunuchs and perverts. "They don't do it to each other," he said. "They do it to machines. That's what I heard—machines! Can you beat that? Why, that's disgusting!"

"When I was a lad, we had the run of all north Cambridge and parts of Somerville," O'Connor told me yesterday. "We held the north bank of the Charles all the way down to the sewage works, and inland to the old Central MTA station." He perched on the end of my cot while I stood at the window, arms folded, in my customary pose of indifference. "Them were the days," he said.

"We had our own turf. But now—man, you see what they've done to us? Thrown us all together here, regardless? Hunkies and wops and nigs and Polacks all mixed up in the same place with us? With *us*. Why, we used to *run* this town. Hell, the entire state, too. And now we don't have a patch of earth to call our own!" He cast me a look of indignation, as if expecting me to share his outrage at this state of affairs. "Oh, we've protested, we've complained, we've done every damned thing we can think of—and so have the others, I'll say that for them, they don't like it any more than we do—every dog wants his own kennel, as the saying goes—but they say they can't oblige us, there aren't enough of us to justify the trouble and expense, so we have to stay packed in here like creatures in the Ark, like it or not. And I can tell you it's a job to keep all hell from busting loose among us—and now and again there's a shindy when the young fellows get their blood up, not that I blame them, the provocations that go on—and a couple of ursids have to come in and lay about them to restore the peace..."

With some difficulty I was able to make some sense out of what he was saying. It seems that the colony consists of the descendants of certain groups which settled in this area centuries ago, living in a state of intermittent warfare. How long this primitive age lasted I have no idea. My knowledge of early American history is skimpy, and my attention wandered frequently during O'Connor's accounts of ancient battles. In any event, the numbers of these tribes dwindled in modern times with the fall in the birthrate, migration, and what O'Connor called "defections"—his term for those who were able to enter our evolving society as free citizens.

They are aborigines. None comes from the outside world. All descend from the original tribal enclaves—and it occurs to me that, as such, they are not really excluded. They have never been "included."

SEPTEMBER 29

How long will I be kept here? This is the important question—the one I have to contain within myself when O'Connor pays me his visits. The man surely is aware of my need to know the answer, for he is intelligent enough, despite his crudity and ignorance, but he has made no reference to my future until today, when something he said implied that my stay here might not be a short one.

Every Saturday, he said, the young men play a soccer game in the open space between the buildings, contests which are supervised by ursids, who frequently have to intervene to break up riots both on the field and among the spectators. "You got the heft to make a pretty good fullback, Fowke," he remarked, casting a judicious eye over me. (I could have told him, if I hadn't sworn not to speak, that no civilized person has engaged in competitive athletics for nearly a century.)

"I wouldn't mind knowing," he added slyly, "which side you'll be on." This remark bothered me. Did it mean he was confident that sooner or later my resistance would break down, and I would accept membership in the colony? He kept peering at me, apparently trying to fit me into one of the aboriginal categories. "You sure don't look Irish," he said. "You've got red hair, all right, but you're a bit dark in the skin, and your nose, it's sort of like a Polack nose . . ." He went on with his personal comments, which tried my patience, although I don't suppose he intended any offense. "If I had to guess, I'd say you were closest to being a Dutchman, I mean you got the build of one, big and wide, you know? And then there's your name. Fowke—that's got a Dutch sound to it. Dutch or Kraut. We had a Dutchman here once, could have been your cousin, except his skin was light and he was blond on top. He was our fullback, not too fast on his feet, but strong. Anybody got in his way he'd go right through 'em. Dutch—that's what we called him, 'Dutch'—he had no head for booze (we brew up a vat now and then). Two cups, and he went wild. He broke through the north fence once. It took three ursids to down him, he was that powerful. And then one day when he'd had a few, he took a run at the south side—know what I mean? Where there ain't no fence? Where they got that other thing you don't see? My God, when he hit it, it sounded like an elephant's fart, and there was a little cloud of mist in the air for a minute—a reddish sort of mist with white streaks in it—and then it blew away in the breeze, and that's all there was left of the man, God rest his soul."

I am back in the dark ages. O'Connor said that every so often some "professors" arrive from the outside to study the colony, and I don't wonder. This is a museum of social horrors, not just of the family and its shames and degradations, but also of the larger familial groups of the tribes, each clinging to its own set of biological and sociogeographic accidents.

OCTOBER 1

Escape is impossible. What happened to the man they called "Dutch" would be proof enough, if I hadn't seen the security devices with my own eyes.

I can't stand the thought of staying here for long. Surely they don't intend to keep me—and yet there has been no indication that I will be sent elsewhere.

That Dutchman must have been like me—a true excluded—and I wonder if I will meet the same end, trapped in this place until I rot or go insane and resolve to be done with this torment by plunging into the electrovallum's field of force?

I must do something to get out. Anything.

OCTOBER 3

I have decided to break my silence. I will speak to O'Connor today. He is my only chance. I've got to win his confidence and sympathy and persuade him to help me escape.

OCTOBER 4

I have to be cautious with O'Connor. I don't want to raise the question of escape too soon.

I have been talking to him about the outside world, telling him about the Juvenor, the Librex system, neural art, etc. From his skeptical reaction, I would judge he thinks I am making most of it up—and why wouldn't he? He knows nothing about what lies beyond his direct experience and observation. The colony is his universe. He doesn't care about anything else. The others don't either. If the ursids were to knock down the fences and depart, I have the feeling these people would stay where they are, prisoners of their own ignorance.

How can I get through to him—how can I convince him to help me?

OCTOBER 5

The Wall—that's the answer. Why haven't I thought of this before?

I've begun telling O'Connor about the Wall. It's hard to believe, but he's never heard of it, and he listened to me with an expression of doubt on his crafty face, as if this were the wildest of my fantasies.

The frustrating thing is that if this colony were a few dozen kilometers to the east, the Wall would be in sight.

In the afternoon I persuaded him to let me go outside for some air and exercise, and while we were there, I continued my explanation of the Rampart System, making a crude diagram of it with dirt and pebbles. Several other people gathered around, watching me with amusement as I crouched there scratching lines in the earth.

I must admit that, to someone with no knowledge of history or technology, the concept of a gigantic barrier system holding the Atlantic at bay is bound to sound like moonshine. O'Connor listens to me, and asks questions—shrewd questions for the most part—but I don't know what he really thinks.

OCTOBER 6

Today I told him about the seepage and how the Wall was probably undermined in several places—and that in the next few weeks or months the ocean might come exploding in across the Shelf with unimaginable force, to tear into the old coastal zone.

His only reaction was to scratch himself under the arms.

"You people are trapped here," I said. "You may think you're safe, but you're not. Boston would be wiped out in a few seconds. The whole metropolitan area would be swept clean."

He squinted at me, gnawing thoughtfully on his lower lip. "A flood, you say?"

"It would be the biggest flood ever."

"And how come you heard about it?"

"I told you. I used to be in charge of the Wall east of Baltimore."

"Baltimore? Hell, that's a long way from here."

"Yes, but the whole system would be involved. Think of it as a big dam. If there's a breach in one part of a dam, pretty soon the entire thing starts breaking apart..."

I went on as patiently as I could, explaining things to him, and he seemed to understand and to be impressed, but of course I couldn't be sure.

"Listen," he said finally, "if there's something wrong out there, they'd move us away. They wouldn't keep us here."

"The problem is that they don't realize what's happening."

"The government doesn't know? Hell, man, they're supposed to know everything."

"Well, they don't know about this."

"So you're saying you're the only one who does?"

"As far as I know, I am."

He gave me a long look but said nothing.

"That's why I've got to get out of here, O'Connor. I've got to get in touch with the top people and tell them what I found out, understand? Then they can do something about it."

I may have gone too fast for him, but I was getting desperate after two weeks in that little room, listening to the racket of that colony of aborigines around me and obsessed by the idea of the swelling force of that crazy giant ocean out there, while this one man held my fate in his hands—my fate and the Wall's. It's true, I'm the only one who knows, who cares, who believes—the only one who has a chance to save it.

He was worried, I could tell. There was a sheen of perspiration on his forehead, and he kept his eyes on me all the time.

"What about it, O'Connor? Can you help me get out?"

He edged back to the door, which I noticed he had left ajar this time. I could have walked right out—not that it would have done me any good.

"I'll think it over," he muttered, and then he slipped out, and the door was closed and locked again.

OCTOBER 7

Usually he shows up in the early afternoon, but he didn't today. By dusk I was getting impatient, and with a couple of kicks I smashed a panel in the door, ready to leave on my own. But then I thought better of it and cleaned up the splinters before they brought my evening meal and decided to wait another day.

OCTOBER 8

O'Connor appeared in mid-morning, his eyes wary and his face grim. He glanced at the broken door panel but didn't say anything about it.

"Well?" I said.

"There's a place where you can get under the fence," he said, his voice low. "It's at the northwest corner. Know where that is? Where the fence angles? Well, we had a dog once that dug his way under—after a bitch, I guess—and we covered up the hole, but the dirt is soft there, and you can dig it out again in a couple of minutes."

"I'm bigger than a dog."

"There's a shovel or two in the tool shed. Pick one up on your way, and you'll have no problem."

"What about the guards?"

"They don't see anything low down to the ground. It's somebody climbing over the top they look for. If you crawl flat once you get through, they won't spot you. They didn't see that dog. We were all there watching, it was broad daylight, and they didn't so much as blink when he skinned under."

"All right . . . but when? Tonight?"

"Sure—tonight. Just wait until the lights go out, and everybody is asleep . . ."

OCTOBER 9

I was agitated and excited, and I had doubts, too—maybe I was expecting too much of O'Connor—but I reasoned that he wasn't risking anything himself, telling me about that place under the fence. Besides, what choice did I have?

The lights went out at half-past ten, and the barracks settled down bit by bit for the night. When all seemed quiet, I tried the door. It wasn't locked. He hadn't thrown the bolt when he left.

Enough moonlight came in from the window at the far end of the corridor for me to find my way to the stairs. I crept down in my socks, carrying my shoes. Once outside in the frosty air, I put my shoes on, went to the tool shed and groped around until I found a spade to take along with me.

Figuring that the ursids on fence patrol might make visual sweeps of the area, I decided to crawl, even though that was hard on my hands and knees and took time. I was winded when I got to the northwest corner, but I didn't stop to rest; I slid down into the perimeter ditch, tumbling in a heap at the bottom.

I got up, ready to scramble up the other side and start digging my way under the fence.

That was when they grabbed me.

One ursid clamped my arms, the other got my legs, and I was dragged back up the slope.

A van had driven up, and another ursid pulled the rear doors open.

Before they tossed me inside, I got a glimpse of O'Connor standing not far away, watching.

I was too stunned to feel anything. Even now, an hour or so later, I'm not angry at him for what he did—he just wanted to get rid of me, having come to the conclusion I was crazy, with my raving about a Wall and a flood.

So here I am, recording all this with my micropen, wondering what's going to happen now. I have no idea where they are taking me, but I think the direction is north.

PART FOUR

NOVEMBER 19

It is the mid-morning break. I am sitting on a heap of gravel in the middle of the Sable Island flatlands. The Wall is a couple of kilometers east. The wind is blowing down from Labrador across the Gulf of St. Lawrence. It has a freezing bite.

From where I sit I can see several other men taking a rest among the rocks and heaps of half-frozen earth, sipping coffee from the containers the murid has brought around. We are warmly dressed in heavy worksuits, caps and gloves, but that bitter wind burns our faces. Frostbite is not uncommon among us.

The nearest man is twenty meters away, the required interval. Prisoners are forbidden to speak; anyone caught at it gets a black mark in his book. We are not even supposed to exchange glances.

Now the coffee murid seems to be studying me, as if registering the movements my hand is making with the micropen. I'll have to slip it back into my boot; the break is almost over anyway.

* * *

I don't know why I've begun writing again after this long interval—it must be six weeks now—but it can't be because I have some hope. I have no more hope than I had when they dumped me here. It may be simply that I've gotten used to desperation.

Or that today is my "birthday"—to use the old-fashioned and inexact word.

I am fifty-seven years old.

NOVEMBER 21

This camp is near the northern terminus of the Wall.

A few kilometers north is what they call the Hinge—where the Wall bends west and runs some two hundred kilometers to Nova Scotia, blocking the Strait of Canso as it hooks onto the continent.

On clear days—and there aren't many of these—I can see the faint outline of this great bend in the Wall in the distance.

It is the Hinge that takes the worst pounding, getting not only the direct force of the Atlantic but also the fierce currents beating down from Newfoundland.

At this point the Wall is more than two hundred meters thick and protected by a double breakwater.

I saw it from the air a few years ago, and it is an impressive sight—like an enormous muscular arm, defensively crooked, its elbow thrust into the throat of the sea. In the dead of winter it is battered ceaselessly by the ice floes that splinter on the breakwaters, sending enormous spears of ice hurtling against the main barrier.

We are digging drainage channels through the flatlands to carry runoff into an existing trench system south of here. As an engineer, I know this project is pointless. Eliminating a few pools of surface water here won't make the slightest difference.

If they really needed surface drainage, they would provide proper equipment: grapplers and servoscoops. Instead, we are working with antiquated draglines and cats and gasrollers. Picks and shovels, too.

The truth is that this is make-work in a punishment camp.

* * *

It is snowing. There are soft streaks across the window of my cubicle where the snow is catching, holding, building—a silent storm, as if the weather, too, were obeying the rule of silence. We cannot even talk to ourselves. On only one occasion have I heard a human voice here. That was when a fellow went out of control and began singing and shouting—he was somewhere in this barracks—and at the end he gave a scream, I guess when the ursid got to him. After that, nothing. Sometimes at night you can hear little cries and mumbles, the kind of sounds men will make in their sleep, but if you do too much of that, it counts against you, even though it is involuntary.

NOVEMBER 22

On the walls of my cubicle are marks left by previous occupants— dim scratches on the hard surface, which must have required hours of effort, since prisoners are stripped of anything which might be used for digging or cutting: belt buckles, pointed or metallic objects of any kind. How could they have done it? With their fingernails, maybe. Or with a chip of stone smuggled in from outside.

There are some initials, a few dates—SWG, 6/8/49...JGS, 8/10/64...but no words, no messages. What words could pierce this silence? Who would receive the messages? Just the initials: JR, CWB, DC. I wonder what happened to them. And what will happen to me.

This northern sky is like the roof of the world, curving out of sight toward the Arctic, bleached by the fierce polar winds; it makes everything down here look small: lumps of earth and stone whitened by snow, the crusty tracks of the draglines and cats, the tiny figures of men dark against the drifts.

Every day I count the number of men I can see. Usually it's

from forty to sixty. Today it's more than eighty. One day last week it was close to one hundred.

This is a big project. It stretches as far as the eye can see across the flatlands parallel to the Wall. Our barracks houses at least fifty men, and there are seven other barracks in sight from here, maybe more elsewhere. The prisoners in this camp must number a thousand, could be twice that.

I don't remember the official figures on the total excluded in this country, but it is something like twenty-five or thirty thousand—and most are supposed to be living in regular settlements scattered through the West.

Is it possible this camp holds such a large proportion of the national excluded population?

I never heard anything about the existence of a punishment camp.

Another accident yesterday. It may not have been an accident. I was too far away to see what happened. I heard clanging metal, a shovel knocking against a rock, which is the trouble signal, and then our section ursid went bounding past me, and a few minutes later I saw it moving toward the camp center carrying a man. I could see an arm dangling down. I worked my way over toward the place and saw red snow and a pick lying there, one of its points rusty-looking, stained. I don't see how a man could fall on his own pick unless he did it deliberately.

There are several accidents a week. I never know what happens to the men who are hurt, or if they live or die.

NOVEMBER 24

Once a month they run us through a stimulator (to relieve tensions, presumably)—my turn yesterday—but it is far from pleasant. They make you strip, and then with two big ursids standing there glaring at you, you enter the envelope, which is clammy from other men's bodies—clammy and worse—and they jack up the settings, so the force of it explodes through you, and it is finished in maybe a minute, and then you get out, shaking all over, and get dressed while the ursids make little whining sounds, which mean hurry up, next man waiting.

NOVEMBER 25

The silence makes me anxious to hear sounds. Any sounds—a footstep, the closing of a door, a sneeze.

Solitude was different outside. I could communicate with anyone anywhere whenever I wanted, with information and entertainment and pleasure at my fingertips. My dignity and independence were protected and enhanced by solitude...but here I am locked within myself. What is going on in this camp? Nothing filters through, no news, no rumors, not even the shadow of someone else's thought. This is the kingdom of solitude; the track-robots rule here.

DECEMBER 2

Being within sight of the Wall gives me courage. I tell myself that as long as the Wall endures, so will I. It may be stupid to think this way—to feel a sense of identity with that mass of rock—but stupid or not, all I have to do is lift my gaze and see its vast bulk through the mist of windblown snow and the fierce cold that makes my eyes water and freezes my lashes stiff and claws through my coat and boots, and there comes a surge of hope, of defiance, of a determination to survive.

DECEMBER 19

Yesterday the ursids piled some forty of us onto a skiwagon and hauled us to the main pumping station at the Hinge.

The entry doors, set in the base of the Wall, were frozen shut, resisting even the savage strength of the ursids. A felid finally had to come with a heatbeam to scorch the ice away.

We stood waiting in the bitter cold with the wind picking up tiny icy granules of snow and swirling them around in little stinging clouds. The others kept their heads lowered to protect their faces, but I looked up at the Wall. It was the first time I had been close to it. This northern Wall has no moss, no lichen; at least there is none visible. There may be microscopic plant life on it of some kind, although it is hard to see how anything could survive the cold and the wind. The rock is scoured bare, which makes it appear new, as if just put in place and not yet settled in. The only thing that manages to maintain a foothold on it is ice. There are sheets of it near the top—from blown spray, I guess—and this makes the Wall glitter when the sun hits it, and it looks like a gigantic iceberg towering to the sky. It is dangerous to come as close as we were, for now and then huge icicles crashed down, some the size of flagpoles. Nobody seemed to notice this, or if they did, they didn't care.

When they finally got the doors open, we were led into a long and downward-canted passageway, slick with ice. Men kept slipping and falling. Even the guards went down. The cold was so intense the air itself seemed frozen. After a few minutes of skidding and stumbling, we came to the pumping room, the size of two tennis courts and as silent as death. Nothing moved, nothing worked; there was no hum of energy in the machines, no scattering of lights across the panels. Everything was iced over. Water had gotten in, probably through a ruptured pipe, and it had frozen, splitting tubes and cracking glasstic and caking over the pumps themselves. Even the fixed felids were encased in ice, like huge moth larvae in transparent chrysalises, staring out at us with their squinty grins.

Our job, it seemed, was to de-ice the place—an impossible task. We had no proper equipment, just that one beam, plus our picks and shovels. Even if we'd all had beams, what use would it have been? The melted ice would have refrozen. All we could do was hack halfheartedly at the stuff, doing more harm than good, since we couldn't help damaging tubes and pump housings and whatever else was within range of our picks. The ursids didn't seem to care. It was just another make-work project, although I suppose that it had once been planned and attempted in various ways, and then when nothing worked, the job slipped down notch by notch on the maintenance scale until it was as good as forgotten. Obviously, by then another unit would have been built elsewhere to do the work.

It strikes me as strange that they would have put a pumping station in this location. I don't know of any others actually within the Wall—they are in the flatlands or at the base of the Rampart— but perhaps they did it because the Wall offered greater protection against the weather up here.

DECEMBER 21

Another day chopping ice down there. We sweat, and the sweat freezes. The air is bad, and there is a claustrophobic sensation of being trapped in that ice chamber in the depths of the Wall.

I can hear the ocean pounding down there. Maybe it's just the blood beating in my ears as my lungs labor for air.

That machinery puzzles me. It is of an antiquated design, and that's no surprise, for I recall that the Hinge was one of the early Wall sections to be built, maybe a century ago. I can't see, looking the system over, how it functioned. There doesn't seem to be any discharge group, although it may have been wrecked in an earlier attempt at salvage and dismantled.

It almost looks as if this station was designed not to pump *out*, but to pump *in*.

DECEMBER 23

We spent our last day inside the Wall yesterday.

The men were getting sick from exhaustion and oxygen insufficiency—dizziness and nausea—and finally the felid registered the situation and had the ursids take us up to ground level.

Today we didn't go back.

* * *

It isn't a pumping station. I know what it is—what it *was*, I mean, because it is nothing now, a flooded-out frozen-over beaten-up useless heap of junk—and maybe I knew it the moment I laid eyes on it. I just couldn't believe what I saw. I wouldn't admit it. I had to see it as a pumping station and to convince myself it was nothing more than that, so if it wasn't working, if it hadn't been working for I don't know how many years, decades maybe, it wouldn't make any real difference.

It is part of the Deeps. It must be that. There is no other explanation for it.

The early Deep sections were built just below the hydroslope; the later ones were sunk farther down . . . deep Deeps.

McKay said the Wall would last a thousand years, but it is failing here, failing at Baltimore Canyon, failing God knows where else, and either they don't know or they don't care or they are helpless to do anything about it.

I saw an escape attempt at noon today. The snow is deep now, more than a meter, and higher where the wind piles it up. The prisoner evidently tried to elude surveillance by burrowing mole-like within one of these hillocks of snow, following its northward slant. At a certain point—he was a hundred meters past the work-line then—he clawed his way to the surface (maybe he was suffocating) and ran clumsily away. I can't imagine what desperate hope he may have had. Maybe he figured if he could get to the Canso Station he could get help, not knowing that the Canadians repatriate our excluded, as we do theirs. It was strange, but the men seemed to be aware of his escape before the guards were. We didn't actually see him at first, at least I didn't, but there was a flush of excitement in the air, like a strong scent—I don't know how to explain it, maybe we have developed a special sensitivity which TRs lack—and while we continued the motions of work, our attention was focused on that dark distant figure thrashing through the waist-high snow.

And then the zone murid made its count-sweep, registered a minus, and signaled the nearest ursid.

The man had no chance. The ursids up here are built for snow. They can leap where the stuff is soft and glide where it's hard, and they cover ground even faster than ordinary police ursids. It was agonizing to watch that thing bounding across the snow like some giant hare, the distance between it and its quarry shrinking fast, and then it reached him and caught him up by the back of his jacket, the way you'd grab a cat by the scruff of its neck, and came bounding back at a slower pace with the poor devil dangling in the air, kicking his arms and legs.

DECEMBER 24

An astonishing event today. I still can't quite believe it.

It rarely happens that anyone comes here from the outside world—I don't mean new prisoners, for we have plenty of those. I mean people who visit for one reason or another and then go away again. Back in October some engineers came in by hover to look at the project. They had no interest in prisoners. In November two people went skimming around in a ski car investigating I don't know what—rabbit tracks or wind patterns in the snow. There isn't much else to look at.

Today there arrived a group of security people, six of them, wrapped in overcoats and scarves. When I saw their square caps, I knew they were from the DIPS. I cast surreptitious glances at them as they prowled around with the straw-boss felid, their breaths steamy in the cold air, stamping their boots in the snow. Perhaps that escape attempt had brought them up, to see if the security needed tightening up, although it's hard to see how it could get tighter than it is.

They were walking toward the place where the prisoner started his futile little tunnel in the snowbank, and the felid was explaining things in his scratchy whiny voice, when I had a rush of what I thought at first was fear, a paralyzing icy flash that froze me stiff, and then I knew, knew more by intuition than anything else, because I couldn't see them except as bulky figures trudging across my line of sight—knew that one of them was a woman, was Julia—and I knew that she knew I was here and which one I was.

I went on making the motions of work—they don't care what you do as long as you keep moving, and it's so cold we have to move—and I was staring at the group of DIPS agents from under the bill of my cap, staring until my eyes watered and I had to blink and dry them with the back of a glove so my eyelashes wouldn't freeze, while questions burst in my mind—what was she doing here? Why had she come?

They moved on, and I couldn't see her any longer. She was lost in the group. I wondered if I'd made a mistake, if she wasn't there at all, if I'd invented her out of my misery and loneliness—how could I have recognized her at that distance and under those conditions?—and then they came back, retracing their steps, nearing me again, and at a certain point she paused, stooping as though to tighten a strap on her boot, detaching herself from the rest of them. She straightened up, looked my way. Seemed to smile.

That was all. Just a moment. Then she walked on, rejoining the others, and they were soon gone from sight. In a few minutes I heard the roar of their snowcar from somewhere behind the sheds, a roar that steadily diminished as the car sped away—I glimpsed it as a dot speeding across the white plain.

I went over to where she'd stood when she adjusted her boot, hoping she'd left a sign, a mark, anything, but I found nothing except trampled snow, footprints going in different directions, leading nowhere.

A look, a smile (maybe a smile).

I can think of nothing else. Why did she come? Was it because of me, was it sheer chance, was it really Julia? She must have gotten herself transferred to the nearest DIPS station; maybe she had been promoted to inspector rank. But why here, why now?

It may have been mere curiosity.

No—it wouldn't be that, she wouldn't go to all that trouble just for that.

DECEMBER 26

I have cast up in my mind that scene in the snow so often I am confused, tormented by doubt. I see her face clearly at times, and then again I see a stranger, can't be sure that figure bundled in the overcoat and scarf is a woman.

Even if she remembers me and wonders about me, even if she wanted to see me, she would have known that coming here would have been pointless. She couldn't help me, she could only catch that glimpse of me, and it would have been depressing to see a man trudging around in the snow in this desolate place, and beyond that, knowing that the sight of her would raise my hopes, it would be cruel. Wouldn't she know that? Because there is no hope for me.

DECEMBER 28

Without warning today two ursids escorted me to the camp center and marched me into some sort of board room: a long table with four felids sitting behind it.

I was worried, thinking this must be the disciplinary tribunal, about to add months to my sentence for whatever rules I had broken, and I stood before the table glum and sullen, with an ursid right behind me.

The felids sat immobile, evidently waiting for the presiding officer to arrive so that the proceedings could begin, although I noticed that there was no chair set out for him.

After several minutes had passed, there entered a murid carrying a small box, which it placed on the table. One of the felids fiddled with the back of the box, and a voice emerged—a rich, deep and resonant male voice, crisp with authority, calling the meeting to order.

I was so confused and surprised I didn't understand what it

was saying. It was some kind of strigid, half the size of the one I'd drowned in the Missouri. It had just one lens, not two, and its antennae were mere bulges.

I had expected a human, one of my kind. I hadn't seen any humans in the camp (apart from visitors, and of course the prisoners themselves), but I had never doubted that there were men and maybe women in the top positions—camp commandant, security chief. Now I suspected there wasn't a single one, and I stood there blinking and swallowing, trying to follow what the strigid was saying in its vibrant male voice with a domineering certainty in it, the voice of one accustomed to command unchallenged. I had the feeling that there was some terrible mistake—that I had the right to be judged by a human creature—that the presence of a living being was absolutely necessary, not for the validity of these proceedings, but for some deeper reason—and my throat began to close and my vision to blur, and I must have swayed, because I felt the ursid steady me with one grip on my shoulder, and I struggled with myself to stay upright and not give way to the impulse I had to roar and lash out against them all. I told myself it didn't matter, laws were laws, and a human judge would follow them, too, and deliver interpretations and rulings that would differ not a whit from a strigid's, and perhaps the strigid would be more just, since it had no glimmerings of mercy and compassion in its breast, whereas a human might seek to quell such latent feelings by being unduly harsh, but still I couldn't help wishing that a human sat where the strigid was, someone with hair and eyes and hands, a living breathing being. Even when it began to dawn on me that the strigid was pronouncing the end of my stay in punishment camp and my imminent transfer to a regular excluded settlement in Kansas, I felt not so much relief and gratitude—well, I suppose I did feel that, although how can you feel grateful toward something the size and shape of a shoebox?—I felt, instead, defeated.

Afterward it occurred to me that maybe Julia had managed to get this transfer for me.

JANUARY 18

The Kansas settlement is a peculiar place, but it is restful after Sable Island. And warmer.

We live in the old town of Ulysses in the southwestern part of the state. It is like stepping into the past, since the government restored the houses and stores and streets the way they were two or three hundred years ago.

JANUARY 21

The indoctrination period took several days. If I listed all the rules and regulations I was supposed to memorize, it would choke the micropen. I didn't pay close attention, being worn down from punishment camp—I must have lost twenty kilos up there—but I figure I just need to do what the others do, and I'll be all right.

We have to wear old-fashioned clothes and follow a strict daily schedule minute by minute, and if you have occasion to speak to other excludeds, only certain topics are permitted—mostly the weather, food and health.

The strangest part is that I have been assigned to live in a house as the male adult member of a family, with a "wife," no less, and two "children."

One of the children is a murid, costumed like a little girl, with a polka-dot dress, a wig and a mask.

It is this creature that monitors the rest of us.

JANUARY 25

The reconstructed part of town is not large—six square blocks, at most—and this is the limit of the settlement, guarded by uniformed police ursids masked and wearing dark glasses, so well disguised that I went up to one to ask directions and got within a couple of paces before I realized what it was.

My weekday schedule goes like this: I get up at seven o'clock and eat breakfast (my "wife" fixes it for me), then I drive to the center of Ulysses in a reproduction antique automobile (a 1952

Plymouth), park it across from the courthouse and go to my office, on the second floor of one of the buildings that line the square. It is supposed to be a real estate office and has period furnishings: telephone, hatrack and typewriter, plus a large colored photograph of President Eisenhower on the wall. There I pretend to work, now and then using the telephone to make imaginary calls or typing phony letters on the typewriter. My performance is monitored by a control within Eisenhower's picture. If I slack off, the President's eyes start flashing at me. At noon I go down for lunch at a "diner," where I eat with several other excluded men who are supposed to be lawyers, merchants, the county judge, etc., and we talk about our health and the weather under the eye of a felid waitress in a frizzy blonde wig. There is a picture of President Eisenhower on the wall there, too.

The afternoon is the same as the morning. At 5:30 I drive the Plymouth "home" again. My "wife" and I talk about our health and the children's health and the weather, and she fixes supper and puts the children to bed—well, the little boy, anyway (he is real)—and we sit in the living room listening to music on the radio (three or four popular songs of the period, played over and over) while she knits and I pretend to read the paper, a facsimile of the Kansas City *Star* dated October 7, 1954, which is never changed. At ten, we go to bed.

On Saturday mornings, I take the children to a little park where they play on swings and slides, and in the afternoon I listen to a radio broadcast of a baseball game—the same damned game, every Saturday. On Sundays we go to the Lutheran church on the corner, and then we come home to eat a big dinner and take naps.

We are evidently rehearsing for a visit by some big-shot tourists, so they can see a living reproduction of small-town life in this historical period, but I wish they'd come and get it over with, so we could relax the rules a little.

JANUARY 30

My wife is a pretty little woman with a timid manner and a fixed, nervous smile. Her name is Shirley—I mean the name assigned to her—and mine is Tom. The little boy is called Danny. He is about eight years old and must be viviparous, as I cannot believe that a child that young would be excluded. It has occurred to me that Shirley may really be his mother. He clings to her, and she comforts him in an anxious way, keeping an eye on me, as if I might disapprove. The two of them are afraid of me, even though I have done nothing to alarm them.

And they are terrified of the little "girl." Whose name is Sandra.

JANUARY 31

I now realize that tourists have been visiting us all along—not many, and they come one at a time—and it is hard to tell at a glance, for they are dressed in period costume, as we are, and don't speak. They just stroll around town looking at us. A fellow came up to my office a couple of days ago and stood in the doorway watching me for a while—I knew better than to speak to him—and then he gave a contemptuous little smirk and went away. Yesterday evening a woman walked right into our living room without a word, looking at everything with a sort of amused distaste. Shirley bent over her knitting, pretending not to notice her. I was ready to say something, but Sandra was glaring at me, and I knew I shouldn't, so I just hid behind the goddamned Kansas City *Star* until the visitor had left.

FEBRUARY 3

It is Saturday noon. I am sitting on the front porch. It is cold and windy. There are sixty centimeters of snow in the yard, where little Danny and his "sister" are playing catch, as required by the schedule. Sandra never misses the ball. Once Danny threw it wildly—it must have gone a couple of meters over her head— and she leaped up and caught it easily. It was uncanny to see that bewigged child-sized creature bound up like that, her steel calves flashing in the sunlight.

Danny and I are cold. We would be inside now if we didn't have to stay out here—he plunging back and forth in the snow, poor little fellow, his nose and ears red with cold, and me shivering in this chair with my hat pulled low. My fingers are numbing. I can barely operate the micropen. Sandra isn't wearing her coat. She doesn't need it. She is dressed, as always, in a summery frock, with long sleeves to cover her upper extensors.

I can see other houses and other yards along the street, and everywhere it is the same: the man sitting on the porch watching a real child and a murid-child playing in the snow.

We all do the same things at the same time.

Shirley and I sleep in the same room, in twin beds. When I first came here, she was frightened of me all the time, but particularly when we went to bed. I don't suppose she slept at all the first couple of nights for fear I might make a sensory approach (and it may be that my predecessor—who is never mentioned, but I am convinced there was an earlier "Tom"—it may be that he tried that, and it could have been the reason why he was removed). I have taken pains to soothe her fears, and she is easier with me now, but I still alarm her, perhaps by my size and the legacy of lumps and scars I bear from what that court ursid did to me last fall.

Flesh contact is not explicitly forbidden by the rules, as far as I can recall—we are excluded, after all—but once when Shirley cut her finger in the kitchen I helped bandage her hand, and suddenly Sandra appeared in the doorway with that fixed glare burning at us, and Shirley gave a little gasp and pulled her hands away from mine and finished the bandaging herself.

So it may be that touching, if not strictly prohibited, is frowned on—and outright sex may be taboo. Sandra's presence is enough to drive any such notions out of my head. She and Danny have separate bedrooms, but of course she doesn't sleep and prowls the house at night. I have wakened to see her standing in a corner of the room watching me—her eyes are luminous—and it is a chilling experience.

I have tried in various ways to communicate with Shirley—that is, by raising topics other than the approved inanities of weather and health—but it only frightens her, and with anguished eyes she begs me to stop.

"How long will this go on?" I whispered to her once in the kitchen when Sandra was outside with Danny. Shirley caught her breath and shook her head in warning. I persisted. "Don't you ever get a break—a vacation?"

"It's going to rain tomorrow," she said.

"No, listen. I've got to know. Will they keep us here indefinitely?"

She glanced worriedly around the room. "The radio forecast says it'll rain," she stammered. She probably thought there was an EAR system in the house; she might be right.

"The little boy—is he yours? Are you viviparous...?" I was whispering question after question, not so much wanting information as reaching for some genuine contact, but everything I said seemed to alarm her, so finally I quit.

They say that compassion opens the door to more violent forms of aggression, and perhaps they are right. I have always condemned it, and even now I acknowledge its dangers.

But I pity Shirley, and I pity the little boy. I wish I could comfort them.

And recognizing this, I realize how far I am from the world I used to inhabit.

FEBRUARY 6

There are some benches in the little park across from the courthouse, and these are occupied regularly by elderly men who sit there gossiping about approved topics and reading facsimile copies of the Kansas City *Star*. That is their job in this reenactment of small-town life in the 1950s. Only in heavy snow or pelting rain are they allowed to take shelter in one of the stores.

Each day after lunch, I take a walk around the square for exercise (it isn't required, but it isn't forbidden, either), hardly giving the old loungers a glance, and today I walked by them as usual—I must have recognized him without realizing it—and got as far as the stone fountain in the middle of the square before something stopped me and made me turn and go back.

I went up to his bench—he sat alone, gloomily looking at his copy of the *Star*—and stared down at him.

"Dr. Grandgent!"

The old man goggled up at me. "Who the hell are you?" he said.

I sat beside him. "I'm Fowke, Dr. Grandgent, don't you recognize me? I was the one who came to Baltimore last summer and asked you about the Wall, and you said I ought to see Barney Dragomine."

He didn't seem to remember me, and he wasn't inclined to talk. He stuck his nose in the newspaper and edged away from me and cast suspicious glances at me out of the corners of his eyes. "You're not supposed to be here," he grumbled. "Why don't you go away?"

I kept trying to jog his memory, although I was beginning to think that the old man was so addled by his advanced years and the troubles he must have gone through in his exclusion that he really didn't know who I was. Just as I was about to give up and leave, he gave a sour little chuckle.

"So—you never got to Dragomine, eh, Fowke?" he said. "I might have predicted it. You certainly made a mess of things."

"What do you mean?"

"Careful," he muttered. "One of those damned things is watching us." Across the square, a murid newsboy had stopped and was staring our way. Any deviation from the norm they are tracked for will alert these low-level but efficient TRs. "You'd better leave, Fowke," Dr. Grandgent said. "Otherwise there'll be trouble."

"Just tell me what you—"

He burst out in sudden fierceness: "Haven't you done enough damage to me already, you bumbling idiot? It was your fault they came to interrogate me and destroyed my field and hauled me off like a sack of potatoes! Thanks to you, I'm spending my declining years in these asinine pageants. I've been in three of them already, each more boring and stupid than the one before. What an indignity for a man my age! They dressed me up as a Pilgrim father in the last one. Can you imagine a reproduction of the Plymouth Colony in Webster City, Iowa?"

He was trembling with anger. His hands were crumpling the edges of the newspaper. I didn't want to enrage him further, so I walked off and made a slow circuit of the square. The newsboy watched me for a while and then went on its way, so I returned to the park and paused when I reached Dr. Grandgent's bench again.

"I'll leave you in peace, sir," I said to him, "if you'll kindly tell me what you know about the Wall. I haven't heard any news for months."

The old man sneezed and wrathfully wiped his nose on the sports page. "The Wall, eh? That white elephant! McKay's folly! You'll be interested to know that it's crumbling section by section, as I could have told them it would if they'd asked me!"

"What sections? Baltimore Canyon?"

"There was a breach at East Georgia, so I heard. I don't know about other zones, but you can bet your money the system won't last long, if it hasn't started collapsing already."

"But if East Georgia breached, the whole Wall must be disintegrating!"

"You're forgetting that there's a cross-rampart down there. If the rip was south of it, this would have shunted the surge west across the peninsula into the Gulf, which would mean that half of Florida doesn't exist any more and the rest is an island."

"My God. Where did you hear this, Dr. Grandgent? On the Vidipix?"

"Don't be a numbskull. Officially there's been no trouble. The so-called security systems prove that everything is in working order."

"But surely, if what you say is true, the top people are taking emergency measures to evacuate the population and to activate the Deeps—"

"Don't count on it, Fowke. The top people are just as stupid and lazy as the bottom ones!"

I was deeply shaken by what he had said and glanced around the square, as if expecting to see tidal waves come surging down the streets of Ulysses—but of course all was calm and quiet. A few reproduction automobiles were lumbering by, and a cat sat on the rim of the fountain in the park.

"The only one with any sense is Barney Dragomine," Dr. Grandgent went on. "I tried to reach him myself after you came to Baltimore, but they wouldn't put me through."

"Listen, Dr. Grandgent. You must have heard it wrong about East Georgia. A break of that magnitude couldn't be kept quiet."

"Of course it could! They don't know how to do much, but they do know how to do that!" Dr. Grandgent, flushed and furious, was wadding up the newspaper in his hands.

The other loungers on the nearby benches were becoming increasingly restive. One of them cupped his hands to his mouth and hoarsely whispered: "Don't you know you're supposed to talk about the weather? You danged fool, you're going to get us all in trouble!"

"So you want to hear about the weather, do you?" Dr. Grandgent snapped back at him. "All right! I'll tell you about the weather! It's going to storm, that's what! A big storm's coming! You're going to get wet! Drenched to the skin!"

"Better lower your voice," I cautioned him. Heads were appearing in windows in buildings around the square. Dr. Grandgent flung his *Star* to the ground, got up, and stamped on it. "They can't fix it, Fowke," he said shrilly. "They didn't even figure on fixing it, understand? They built it—and lost interest! The technology leveled off. No, it didn't level off, it stopped! Vanished! The bright boys went off chasing other rainbows—track-robots and bio-synthesizers! Macro-geriatrics! Living historical reproductions!"

I was dismayed and uneasy. Was he right about the Wall? I tried to calm him, but he only got madder. He was kicking the bench. It was clear that my presence enraged him, so I began moving away. "There are no values!" the old man screeched. "No continuity! No follow-through! Everything's surface and shine! Consequences be damned! Don't tell me about the Wall! Tell Dragomine—if you can get to him! But don't bother trying! He couldn't do anything about it now! The whole system is busting apart! Everything! We're sliding into a new Ice Age—!"

I reached the edge of the park and crossed the street, heading for my office. Looking back, I saw Dr. Grandgent dancing on his newspaper, his skinny arms flailing the air. The other old men had prudently withdrawn behind the fountain. I entered my building and went up to the office. From the window, I could see two figures approaching my ex-teacher. The murid newsboy had returned, bringing a uniformed ursid patrolman. I could still hear Dr. Grandgent's squeaky excited voice, although I couldn't make out his words. President Eisenhower's eyes were flashing angrily at me, so I had to turn from the window and go back to my "work," and I didn't see Dr. Grandgent taken away.

FEBRUARY 7

I walked by the old men in the park at noon today and took a look at them, but of course Dr. Grandgent wasn't there. I didn't expect him to be. The loungers glowered at me, as if what happened yesterday was my fault. Maybe it was.

FEBRUARY 10

The days plod by, heavy and mindless and dull. I go to the office and pretend to work, I take the children to the park, I read the October 7, 1954, Kansas City *Star*, while Shirley knits, and we talk about the weather and listen to the radio and its repetitive cycle of songs, as Sandra in her wig and summer frock stares at us from the shadows of the hall. Sometimes a tourist will walk around the house or peer in at a window or enter the living room and look at us the way you'd look at apes in a zoo, but even this is part of the routine and does nothing to relieve the boredom.

"How do you feel today?" asks timid Shirley.

"Fine," I say. "Fine." If I say anything else, it worries her.

This reproduction of life—this facsimile that is always the same, unchanging day by day, week by week—I wonder if it is really the way people lived back then.

At night I lie wakeful, waiting for sleep. I can hear the clock in the Lutheran church tolling the hours. The streetlight through the curtains makes a mottled pattern on the wall. I can hear the little boy when he turns in his bed or coughs, and I am aware of Shirley's wakefulness. She is listening to him, too, and wondering if she should go in to him, but doesn't want to encounter Sandra in the hall. I sigh and shift the position of my pillow, and my thoughts move toward the Wall.

I see it standing against the endless pounding of the Atlantic, a weakened giant, eroded by winter storms and autumn gales, year after year without cease, a forgotten monument to national pride and purpose, left to its destiny. Was Dr. Grandgent right? Was the security system as incapable of sealing as it had proven incapable of giving the alarm? I sometimes feel a physical anguish, as if I am a part of that splendor of sea-battered rock—that overblown dike, as Dr. Grandgent called it once. I have a hunger to see it again, to touch it, climb it, walk it, to lend it what strength I have, for it has been betrayed and abandoned, as I have been. The Wall has been excluded, too.

FEBRUARY 15

The sensation of being watched is so common that I stopped paying attention to it after while, and I haven't felt watched, even though I know I am—watched by Sandra at home, by President Eisenhower at the office, by the felid waitress at the "diner," etc.—

but in the past two or three days I have had the impression that I am being observed by something else, something new, something outside the routine.

FEBRUARY 16

Last night at bedtime I switched off the lights as usual, but before climbing into bed, I parted the window curtains and looked down into the street, which is always empty, and I saw something in the shadows between the streetlamps, where the light doesn't quite reach: a figure, it seemed. Was it looking up at the house— at my window? It didn't move. When I got up to take another look later, it was gone.

I do nothing all day, but I am tired. Lethargy has settled into me. I feel slack and languid. Does this mean I am starting to accept this life? That I will become like Shirley, too worn down and subservient even to entertain the idea of escape?

It is becoming an effort merely to write. And I foresee the day when I will put away the micropen forever. That will be the day of my surrender.

FEBRUARY 17

A tourist entered the house after supper this evening, marching in without knocking in that arrogant way they have, and as we are supposed to take no notice of them, and being used to these invasions by now, Shirley and I didn't look up. But I realized after a few moments that this tourist wasn't nosing around the room looking at things the way they usually do, wasn't moving at all. Glancing around the edge of the newspaper, I saw shoes, ankles, calves, a skirt. I lowered the paper—then dropped it and got to my feet, staring at her. It was Julia.

"I'm on vacation," she said abruptly in a harsh, strained voice— and the sound had a stunning effect, for never had a tourist spoken before. Shirley gave a start and clutched her knitting to her bosom.

Sandra appeared in the hall doorway, her eyes burning behind the slits in her mask.

I was too amazed to speak. The room was suddenly too small, the ceiling too low. I could hear my own breathing. The church bell began to toll the hour, its dull strokes wading through the winter evening, and the three of us seemed held immobile there, waiting for the end. Julia had a tense look; she kept eyeing Shirley strangely. Her posture was defiant and guarded. I stood bemused, my heart racing.

The last stroke sounded. I had counted them. It was nine o'clock.

"Julia," I said. My voice sounded unnaturally loud. Shirley gasped. It was unheard-of, an excluded speaking to a tourist! She gathered up her knitting and went hurriedly out of the room.

Julia looked around impatiently. "Well," she said sharply, but didn't go on. She seemed angry and uncertain and didn't look at me directly. "What's that?" she said, turning toward Sandra in the doorway.

"That's—" I hesitated. Then I laughed. "That's supposed to be my little girl. My daughter."

Julia took a closer look and saw what Sandra was. "Go away," she said, making a shooing motion with her hands. Sandra didn't move. "Did you hear me?" Julia snapped. To my surprise, the murid obediently left, walking backwards.

Julia's appearance had jolted me out of my languor. I felt a surge of vitality, of hope. Why had she come? And why did she seem so sour? She was prowling around in a restless way and still wasn't looking at me. "So this is your home," she said with some contempt in her voice.

"Home? They put me here. You know that."

"You're not so badly off, Fowke. It's better than Sable Island, anyway."

"Did you go up there? Was that you that day?"

She didn't answer. She picked up a knitting needle Shirley had dropped and snapped it in two. She turned to face me. "And that little wife of yours is rather pretty," she said sarcastically. "Don't you think so?" I didn't know what to make of this and didn't

reply. "You certainly don't lose any time at night, do you?" she
added. "Ten o'clock—and bang! Lights out!"

"So it was you out there watching the house—"

"She's up there now, waiting for you. I certainly don't want
to interfere with your domestic pleasures—"

I was astonished. Was it possible she was jealous? "Wait a
minute, Julia. You don't understand!"

"I understand what I see!"

She started for the door. I hurried ahead of her and blocked
the way. "You know I'm a prisoner here," I said. "So is Shirley—
that woman. Do you really think we want to be here?"

"Step aside, Fowke!"

I pushed the door open, letting her pass, and followed her out
to the porch. "We can't talk here," I said. "That murid hears
everything." She went down the steps and out to the street, and
I stayed beside her. "Listen to me, Julia. This place—I can't stand
it. It's destroying me. Another week like this, and I'll be finished."
She was walking quickly along the street but seemed to be listening to me. "Something's happened to my brains," I went on.
"Do you know how many times I have to listen to 'White Christ-
mas' and 'God Bless America'? And read and reread that damned
newspaper? And listen to the same ball game? I'd almost rather
be back at Sable Island."

We had gone halfway down the block. The street was empty.
Anyone outside after dark risked being caught by the cruising
police patrols.

"There's no relationship between me and that poor female back
there, Julia," I said. "I should think that would be obvious. For one
thing, she's indigenous, and probably viviparous, too. She has a little boy you didn't see—he's gone to bed—and I'm convinced he's
hers. I mean, she gave *birth* to him." I paused to let the effect sink
in. "I'm sure you can understand that any connection with her
would be unthinkable for a man of my background."

Julia made no response, but I had the impression that my
explanation was having a mollifying effect on her.

We stopped in the shadow of some trees. The light from the
streetlamps didn't reach us there.

"Why did you come here, Julia?" I said. She made no reply; I couldn't see her face. "You shouldn't risk being seen with me," I said. "You'll get in trouble yourself."

"Don't worry. A DIPS agent can get away with almost anything." She stepped closer. "I came to help you get out of this place."

"How?"

"It shouldn't be hard. I've figured out a way."

I wanted to take her hand but didn't dare. "If I can escape," I said, "I want to go back to Baltimore Canyon."

"You wouldn't have a chance."

"Maybe not, but I want to see the Wall again."

"You've got to get across the border to Mexico. There are hundreds of others down in Chihuahua and Coahuila. You'd be safe for years. The Mexicans extradite a few now and then just for form's sake. They leave the rest alone."

"I don't want to go to Mexico. Not until I've seen the Wall. I heard that there's been a sea-breach in East Georgia. Is that true?"

"I haven't heard anything like that. It hasn't been in the news."

The half-hour struck. It was nine-thirty. The air was chill. I had come out without my coat. She began speaking quickly, with urgency. She told me what I needed to do to escape and insisted I go to Mexico, to Ojinaga, just across the border. She would come there in the spring—she had accumulated leave she would take—and then . . . and then what? This was a question we didn't ask. We couldn't look beyond Mexico, and we stood there silently in the shadows, wondering what might lie ahead.

I could hear the distant rumble of an automobile. That would be the night patrol. In another minute or two it would enter this street to sweep the yards with its searchlight. I had to get back to the house before it arrived, but I couldn't leave her. A storm of tenderness was breaking in me. "Why are you doing this, Julia?"

She hesitated. "You wouldn't be here if it hadn't been for me. You wouldn't have had to go through this."

"It was your job. You shouldn't feel badly."

"I wanted to testify for you at your arraignment, but they wouldn't let me."

We were talking on the surface of what we felt, wanting to say more—at least I did—but holding back, as if these other things could be said only in a language we didn't know.

The sound of the patrol car was louder.

"You've got to go, Fowke. Don't let them catch you out here."

"All right."

"Remember—tomorrow!"

I ran along the sidewalk, bursting into my yard and up the porch steps as the lights of the patrol car swung around the corner. Sandra was standing inside by the living room window, her slitted eyes glowing. I hurried up the stairs to the bedroom, wondering if she had been able to pick up anything of what we had said. Had she sent an alarm signal?

I looked through the curtains down to the street. The patrol car passed by without slowing.

FEBRUARY 19

Everything went as planned—at first.

I got up at the usual hour, ate the breakfast Shirley prepared, went out to warm up the Plymouth, and returned for my briefcase (into which I had slipped two apples and some cheese and bread).

I faced Shirley and the little boy for what I knew was the last time, but of course I could make only the prescribed farewell:

"See you later."

"Have fun," said Shirley.

"You, too."

I felt guilty at leaving them behind, but what could I do? If I brought Shirley along, there was no telling what Julia's reaction might be, and besides, piling my "wife" and "son" into the car with me would have been such a blatant departure from routine that Sandra would have signaled immediately.

I started off in the usual direction for the center of town, but after I had gone two blocks, I turned right instead of left and headed for the southern checkpoint, where a striped pole blocks the street and a uniformed officer stands on duty—but there was no officer now, the pole was raised, and Julia was waiting there with five containers of gasoline, waving impatiently to me as I drew near.

"Hurry," she shouted as I stopped. "He'll be back any minute!" She had managed to send the ursid off on some pretext. I don't know where she got the gasoline or how she arrived at the checkpoint—there was a town taxi, and she may have taken that—but the extra fuel was essential to get me through Texas.

I was about to open my door and get out to help load the containers in the trunk when the officer came tearing out of a side street on an antiquated motorcycle and skidded to a stop just in front of me. Julia ran up to him, pointing in another direction and yelling. This seemed to confuse and slow the ursid but did not stop him.

He tramped up to my car and peered in at me through his dark glasses. Then he began trying to open the door, which I had locked. I held the inside handle with all my might. I knew it would be useless to slip out the other side and try to escape on foot, and if I drove off, he would catch up with me on the motorcycle; even if he didn't, he would give the alarm, and I would be blocked before I'd gone far.

All these considerations flashed through my mind as I sat hopelessly tugging on the handle, waiting for the ursid's superior strength to force the door open. I couldn't see what Julia was doing. I felt something snap inside the door. The ursid had wrenched the outer handle off and stood gazing at it in momentary puzzlement. Then he drew back one gloved grab to smash the window glass—and burst into flame.

What she'd done, I realized a moment later, was to douse him with gasoline and toss a lighted match at him. I shrank from the flash of heat and light. The ursid tottered back, his uniform blazing. Wisps of charred cloth rose into the air. One glove flamed like a torch.

"Get going, Fowke," Julia screamed at me. "I'll have to get rid of the motorcycle." She ran ahead, jumped into the saddle of the cycle and started the engine, waving to me to go ahead. I drove past her, watching in the rear-view mirror as she shot the other way, toward town, cut around the corner and disappeared from my sight.

Then there was a terrific series of explosions behind me and a sea of flame and smoke. I realized that the ursid must have staggered back and fallen where the other gasoline cans were. My fuel supply had blown up—and when the Plymouth ran dry, there'd be nothing for me to do but walk.

The day was clouded and chill; wreaths of mist hung across the road. The Plymouth shook across the pocked and lumpy surface. I drove fast, squinting ahead through a light rain that had begun slanting down. I wondered if there might be other checkpoints up ahead or mobile security units on patrol. After several "miles," as distance was measured on the odometer, the rain began coming down harder, and soon it turned into sleet, which built up at the corners of the windshield. There were slick patches on the road where the car skidded. I had to drive more slowly. It was hard to see ahead now. The sleet was slamming straight at me, and the road, which had been neglected for decades, had no guide-markers at the sides. Once I ran off it entirely into a field, missing a ditch by a hair.

The storm gave me a certain security—whoever might follow me would have trouble finding me in this blinding mess—but it worried me, too, because I couldn't be sure I was headed in the right direction. There were forks and side roads—or what seemed to be side roads—and what before had clearly been the main highway south I couldn't swear I was following any longer. South, west, north, it all looked the same.

It is nearly midnight.

I am sitting half-frozen in the automobile (I can't afford to waste fuel keeping the heater going), waiting out the night.

I have the impression I'm headed the wrong way but won't be in a position to know until dawn. The storm has eased off some, though.

* * *

FEBRUARY 20

It is dawn. The sun has risen behind me. I have been going due west. The road stretches straight as a string toward the far mountains. I am pointed toward Colorado, not Texas.

Maybe there will be a turning somewhere farther on.

It has been years since anyone drove on this highway, if you can call it a highway. The surface is waffled and wrinkled and split a thousand ways, with lumps of tough grass growing out of it and, here and there, a young tree emerging. In places it has disappeared altogether beneath the windblown dirt and sand, or is gouged out by rainwash gullies, full of stones. I came across a road marker once, but it was no more than a shield of rust, and I couldn't read it.

The mountains are nearer—and the fuel gauge indicator is sinking fast. This reproduction Plymouth wasn't built for heavy duty. It is shuddering and rattling, and there is a groan in the engine.

This is empty country. I have passed the ancient ruins of three ranches—rotted fence poles, tumbledown hulks of barns and houses, cow bones scattered in the weeds. Once I went through what had been a little town. It was no more than a junkyard of old planks and broken glass and stone chimneys and bricks chewed by time and weather, with gophers peering at me and roadrunners chasing lizards across my path.

I have one apple left. There is snow in the mountains, so I shouldn't die of thirst, but food is another matter.

My guess is that I have another fifty "miles" left in this shoddy fake antique.

FEBRUARY 23

I am walking in the mountains.

The Plymouth quit near the shell of an abandoned gasoline station. I thought there might still be a little fuel in the underground tank, but of course what was left of the pumps had long since rotted and clogged. The only thing that had survived intact in that place was the ceramic toilet where the bathroom had been.

I wouldn't have been able to drive much farther anyway. The road ended in a big washout up ahead. I tried to find it later, but there were so many landslides and gullies it was impossible.

I have been following a creek now for a day and a half, still heading west. My aim is to reach the Denver-El Paso glassway and sneak a ride south on one of the big transports.

FEBRUARY 25

Last night just before dark I found part of a deer carcass in the snow. I wasn't the first comer; something else had already dined on it, but I wasn't in a mood to be choosy. Built a fire with my last matches and roasted it.

My shoes are giving out.

I saw a big cat at noon today. Probably a cougar. I shied a rock at him, and he didn't even blink.

Before I left the Plymouth, I salvaged whatever I thought might come in handy. With the heelplate from the gas pedal and a chunk of flint, I can strike sparks for a fire, but it takes me about an hour to get a blaze going.

FEBRUARY 27

I dug a snake out from under some rocks and stomped it to death. Just in time. I was weak and dizzy. Didn't wait to make a fire, just ate it raw.

The cougar is trailing me. The bastard must know that I am almost finished.

PART
FIVE

APRIL 4

We are in the San Miguel Mountains in western Colorado, between the Dolores River and Disappointment Creek. There are seventeen of us: eight men, two women, and seven dogs. We are outlaws and fugitives and must be constantly on the move from one cave or thicket to another. We eat whatever we can trap or kill. If it weren't for the dogs to give the alarm and chase down jackrabbits and gophers, we wouldn't last long. We have no weapons except what we have made ourselves: slings and clubs and a crude kind of spear. Dr. Glynn has fashioned a bow and a handful of arrows but hasn't hit anything yet.

I have been with these people for nearly three weeks. I doubt that I would have survived without them, survived this long, that is. Survival is a day-to-day question with us. God knows what will happen to us tomorrow.

* * *

Before I stumbled across Dr. Glynn's band, I had trekked alone through the mountains for what must have been a good two weeks—I lost track of the days—eating snow and tree bark and carrion when I was lucky enough to find any. On the fifth or sixth day after I abandoned the Plymouth, I discovered the wreck of a logger's hut half-buried in the snow and dug a pair of old skis and a rusty axe out of the rubbish. With these I was able to ambush an elderly deer, chase him downhill, get close enough to stun him, and then make my kill. That gave me food for days and skin for foot wrappings and tools from the horns and bones— a sort of knife, honed on rock, and a spearpoint I stuck in the split end of a stick and bound with dried tendons.

The glassway was unreachable. It runs through the plateau country on steel columns fifty meters high, smooth and slick and impossible to climb. I stood looking up at it for a while, listening to the distant hum of traffic, and then I went on my way, thinking I'd be better off finding the headwaters of the Rio Grande, building a raft, and floating south toward Mexico on that—which I tried, and damned near drowned, for the logs parted right after my launch, and I slipped into the icy water, losing my skis and axe. I crawled out on the far bank, stripped off my wet rags, and got a fire going just in time to save myself from freezing stiff.

I don't remember much about the next few days. It was my lowest point. I was getting ready for death, I think. Just dragging myself through the rough country, dizzy from hunger and tortured by an infected tooth.

One morning I came to a clearing and saw a large gray hare thrashing on the ground, squeaking and struggling. I approached and saw that it was entangled in a crude trap fashioned from bent saplings and twisted deerskin thongs. I was about to throttle the hare and make off with it when I heard noises in the underbrush and hid myself. What I thought at first glance were two large animals—bears, walking semi-upright in a stooped position— proved to be men, clad in a patchwork of skins, moving with cautious and fearful steps, as if they expected an attack at any moment and were prepared to flee. They were accompanied by a pair of hairy little dogs, which darted here and there, sniffing and growling. One came right up to where I crouched, gave a short sharp bark, then sniffed me, licked my fingers and, to my relief, dashed away.

The men clubbed the hare to death, disengaged it from the trap, which they reset, and returned the way they had come. I followed them at some distance, being careful to remain out of sight. After twenty minutes or so they reached a campsite on a knoll, where I saw other figures moving around a fire. I observed them for some time, wondering who they were and how they had come to this remote place. They wore a strange assortment of garments, mostly the skins of animals, inexpertly held together. Their faces were darkened by dirt and fire-smoke. The tools they possessed (spears and clubs, primarily) were of the utmost crudity. After my experience in the settlement at Ulysses, my first thought was that this must be another historical spectacle, and although I was drawn to these strange creatures as fellow humans, I was wary of approaching them. Life in Kansas had been bad enough, but to be trapped in a prehistoric village in the wilderness for the amusement of tourists could be worse.

Another night in the open, shivering in the bushes overlooking the camp, made my mind up for me. My bad tooth had given me a fever, and I knew I had to have help or die alone. In mid-morning, I trudged toward the camp, arms raised in a sign of peace and surrender, and was greeted with some suspicion by the people there, who turned out to be not phony actor-primitives, but excluded fugitives like me.

APRIL 5

This is wild rough country, high and forested. The streams run fresh with snow-melt from the mountains, and we fish in the pooled reaches. There are plenty of animals—deer, foxes, goats, bear and wildcats and beaver, but no humans except ourselves.

APRIL 7

The dogs sent up a storm of barks at dawn that roused us scrambling from sleep, grabbing our clubs and spears and rushing into our defensive position—a sort of circle around two boulders where the rock throwers stand. I'm one of them. We waited, trembling with cold, tensed and ready for an attack, watching the dogs, which rushed back and forth barking. The pack leader, a German shepherd we call Boss, darted into the woods, came back, darted in a different way, and then finally he returned and lay down, and the dogs quieted. It hadn't been a false alarm—there'd been an ursid out there somewhere—but its approach had been just a feint, and now it had moved off.

The dogs are incredible. An ursid has no scent and moves so silently you can't hear a leaf rustle, but the dogs never fail to give the alarm. They must detect movement by the displacement of air or by the silences of the birds, I don't know; they have a sixth sense, and they are fearless. They will charge an ursid, dodging its grabs at the last moment, luring it into a pursuit that takes it away from us.

One dog was killed last week that way.

We came on what was left of it in a ravine. The poor beast had been pulled to shreds.

A single ursid we could deal with, I think. Maybe two of them. More than two—I doubt it.

I am convinced they could wipe us out at any time, if they were directed to do it. Four or five of them rushing us simultaneously—it would be a terrible carnage. The fact that they don't indicates that they are merely using us for training purposes. We have the sensation that they know where we are all the time, even when days go by without an alarm. Sometimes we catch sight of one far off—halfway up a slope or standing in a clearing—just watching us.

At least they don't carry weapons—federal law prohibits arming TRs—although those grabs are enough.

And apparently they don't climb trees.

All they have done in the three weeks I have been with Dr.

Glynn's band is to track us and watch us and feign attacks, except we never know whether it will be a real one or not, and it keeps us in a constant state of dread.

Two days ago we came on an elk that had been killed by an ursid.

The head was twisted off. Nothing else would have done that—twisted off the head and left it there for us to find as a macabre warning.

Ferguson, who was a TR programmer before his exclusion, insisted that it must have been an accidental encounter. The elk probably charged the ursid. It's certainly true that a pack of ursids programmed to kill large game would clear out these mountains in no time.

APRIL 8

We have moved higher. There are patches of snow on these slopes, and at night it is bitter cold, but we feel a little safer here than in the forest or down on the plateau. Ferguson thinks these ursids have a mobility loss at freezing temperatures. I didn't mention the snow-ursids at Sable Island.

Last night Dr. Glynn told me what happened to a man named Wright a month or so before my arrival.

The band always hunts in groups of three or four, with some of the dogs, but on this particular morning someone was sick, so Wright went out to check the traps accompanied only by Mc-Partland, and all of a sudden an ursid came thundering through the trees at them—the dogs set up a flurry of barks, but it came so fast the men had no chance to get back to the camp. McPartland had the presence of mind to scramble up a tree, but Wright panicked and ran, while the dogs charged the ursid, snapping and dodging, trying to draw it in another direction. The ursid went speeding straight after poor Wright, and both of them vanished in the underbrush.

That was the last McPartland saw of him. Later, when the dogs let him know there was no immediate danger, he climbed down, ran back to the camp and told the others what had happened, and a search was organized. They followed Wright's trail and found traces of blood in the middle of a thicket and broken branches all around and one of his gloves in a bush, nothing more. The man had disappeared. Did the ursid kill him, and carry the body away? Was he captured and taken back to confinement somewhere? We will probably never know.

I have the impression there are other stories Dr. Glynn could tell me but isn't sure it would be a good idea, thinking I am frightened enough as it is. We are all frightened. This freedom is a terrible freedom. Sometimes it occurs to me that we are simply in a different kind of punishment camp.

APRIL 10

Every day before sunset we lay out our defensive position in case of night attack—a rough bulwark of rocks and branches, which provides a security that is more psychological than real. We build our fire in the middle and cook whatever there is to cook and then, taking guard duty turns, we sleep.

The nights are clear and brilliant. The days grow warmer. The deciduous trees on the plateau below are greening. We have seen more bears—brown bears, luckily. No grizzlies yet. Sometimes cougars come near at night. We can see their eyes reflecting the campfire, red stars in the dark. This stirs up the dogs, but they just growl, so we know it's not an ursid.

Dr. Glynn is very tall—taller than I am, in fact—and as gaunt as a rake handle. He has a long white beard, the end of which he has the habit of tucking into his mouth to gnaw on when he is thinking. He is the leader by tacit consent, perhaps because of his fame as a sociologist. His jottings form part of the basic Librex stock. I can't say he is a practical man—he is dry and academic in manner and confronts daily problems as if they were classroom exercises—but he does his best to keep us in good spirits and seems undaunted by our hardships. Why he was excluded and how he escaped, I don't know.

The range of professional qualifications represented here is broad. We have doctors, microbiologists, physicists, engineers, and technicians like Ferguson, but, unfortunately, experience of the kind needed in the wilderness is virtually nonexistent. Our skills are too high-level to be of use. We are accustomed to a complicated support network of laboratories, information and follow-through systems, felids, etc. Out here we are like children. Such a simple thing as making a fire is at the very limit of our powers. Seligson is an astrophysicist who studied the outer reaches of the universe, where there are no jackrabbits. When it is his turn to skin one, you are likely to get fur in your stew.

APRIL 13

No alarms for a week. What does this mean? Ferguson argues that we should move even higher and dig in—build a fortified camp, with permanent barricades and camouflaged pits to trap attackers. He says we should figure out a way to disable and capture an ursid, so he can take it apart and try to understand its programming. It's an interesting idea, but nobody is volunteering to carry it out.

We keep moving—a day here, a couple of days there. Now we are on the bank of a creek, full of fish, which we catch with rabbit-gut nets.

It would be common sense for us to bundle up together at night for warmth, but the taboo against touching is too strong. Each person shivers alone beneath his or her allotment of pelts. The dogs, mere animals, sleep comfortably in a heap. They also play together; we do not play.

And they engage in flesh-contact sex, the sight of which embarrasses us, but also gives rise to disquieting thoughts. In me, anyhow. I am strongly attracted to Joan Raffy, a geneticist, a large woman who reminds me of Hilda—and I have the impression (which may be wrong) that she is aware of this and is not unaffected by it.

Dr. Glynn sometimes speaks to the group—lectures, actually—about the importance of maintaining the moral and ethical values of civilization.

And yet we are no longer in the modern world. We live in the Stone Age.

APRIL 17

Two ursids at dawn. A terrible attack. We have one dead, two seriously wounded. Three dogs killed.

APRIL 18

They came from different directions—one from above, rushing down the slope, the other charging up from below. This confused the dogs, which ran in circles, barking wildly, and so we, too, were disoriented in those first few vital instants. The one from below veered off just before the barricade, as if it were another feint—it came in from the side moments later, while the other one, the one we didn't see, burst into the camp, broke through our fire, scattering embers, swinging its grabs like scythes, cutting and smashing whatever was in its range. It was horrible. These things run at terrific speed, bent slightly forward, and they can stop and turn with incredible swiftness. Only the most agile dog can elude them. I had seized my sling and sack of stones and had leaped up on my boulder. Everything was clouded by morning mist and smoke from the fire. People were screaming. I still can't remember clearly what happened. Both ursids were pounding back and forth through the camp. I saw a dog—part of a dog—fly through the air, saw somebody's bloodied face whirl by, and felt something sharp cut my side as one ursid whipped past me, slashing. My sling was useless as a sling. I used it as a club,

jumping down from the boulder and swinging blindly in a high
are so I wouldn't hit one of my companions. The attack lasted
perhaps two minutes; it seemed hours, the smoke and mist shattered by screams and racket from the dogs, with those two gray
figures silently wheeling and charging, wheeling and charging,
their long grabs whirring through the air with a chunky slapping
sound whenever they hit something. One loomed up in front of
me. I could see the glint of its lenses as it rushed me—I aimed
for that—and hit it square on. The impact jolted my whole body.
The ursid stopped in its tracks as if stunned, and I swung all the
way around and hit it a second time, lower down, on a grab joint.
It began to move backwards and then off to one side. I started
after it, tripped over something and fell into part of the scattered
fire. When I scrambled up, my jacket smouldering, I saw it running off in a strange way, tilted to one side and dragging one
leg, almost hopping. The other ursid wasn't in sight. And then
mine, too, vanished into the downhill mist.

It was the geophysicist, Mazivo, who was killed. The side of his
head was smashed.

We buried him that afternoon.

Seligson has a dozen of ribs broken, may have internal injuries.
He looks bad. Carl Mackerman has lost a lot of blood from deep
gashes along his left side and arm; he seems to be in shock and
may not live.

The rest of us have lesser injuries—cuts and contusions. Jean
Cady has a broken hand.

Of the three dogs killed, the most serious loss is the leader,
Boss.

APRIL 21

Even in the aftermath of this horror—we are dazed and stricken
and can barely stir ourselves to do essential things—even now, I
say, we remain true to our conditioning. No words of remem-

brance for Mazivo. None for Boss and the other dogs. We may have wept—I know I did—but it was not for them, it was in fear of ourselves.

I tried to say a few words of comfort to Carl and reached out to pat his hand. The man was dying, nearly dead, but with his last ounce of energy, he pulled away to avoid my touch.

The others looked at me strangely, as though I had done something wrong.

I felt a twinge of doubt—I can't quite call it guilt—some little ripple of conscience, realizing that what I did was offensive to him and to the others. Maybe it should have been offensive to me, too.

We have moved up another few hundred meters to a knoll that is more defensible, and we have dug a trench too wide for ursids to leap—at least Ferguson thinks they couldn't.

Carl is sinking, barely breathing. Seligson is in much pain. He whimpers all the time.

We have no medicine. Dr. Zenger does what he can.

APRIL 24

In the morning Ferguson and I went out to check the traps and came across the track that damaged ursid had made, although we didn't know what it was then. It looked as if someone had plowed a narrow furrow in the soil, running straight as a string into some pines. About forty meters into the woods we saw the thing doubled over on one side, lying rigid.

We knew it might still be dangerous. I told Ferguson we oughtn't to take any chances, but his professional instincts were aroused, and he persuaded me to help him try to capture it. We had some gut rope with us and with great caution looped it around the ursid's ankles, if you can call them ankles, and tied it to a couple of stout trees. We knew that a fully operative ursid could have snapped it like a spider web, and we kept an eye on the nearest climbable trees as we worked, holding our breaths.

Our dogs lay down at some distance with their muzzles between their paws, as if they feared the worst and didn't want to see it.

We tied up the grabs the same way—and then came the risky part: trying to detach the head.

Ferguson had made a crude screwdriver out of a belt buckle. With that and his flint knife, he knelt beside the ursid and went to work, while I stood with my club raised, ready to slam it down at the first sign of movement.

We both were dripping with sweat, and every once in a while one of the dogs would groan in anxiety; my arms and shoulders ached from the weight of the club and the tension. But the ursid didn't so much as quiver. Ferguson pried and poked and jabbed, panting with effort and fear. At one point the ursid gave off a hum, which made us jump—but it was a favorable sign. Ferguson had reached the nucloid ganglion. One more cut and it was over. The head wasn't detached, but he said he was satisfied that the connection had been broken, and he gave the ursid a demonstrative kick. The head—that ugly steel gray shell shaped like a football—flopped on one side; the limbs and body remained still.

We dragged it back to camp, and Ferguson eagerly went to work on it, prying off its thoracic and parietal casings.

APRIL 25

I can hear the baying of the wolves from the darkness downhill. I wonder if they have found Mazivo's grave. The night is glorious—the light of the full moon breaking across the peaks and valleys creates a glowing ghostly sea of frozen forms—but we are swept by foreboding and depression. Tomorrow we will dig another grave, for Carl, who died at sundown. How long can we survive? No one speaks of it—in fact, we hardly speak at all—but I know others must be thinking what I am thinking: that we face certain death here, from hunger and exposure, if not from ursid attack, and the only sane thing to do is to work our way east to the nearest settlement and give ourselves up. Even that might be beyond our strength now.

* * *

"Every society in the history of humankind has practiced exclusion," Dr. Glynn said—this was at supper when (except for the two on guard duty) we were by the fire eating roast wildcat, a tough and sinewy dish. "There have been no exceptions, insofar as scholars and researchers know. Only the form of exclusion has differed. In some societies, it has been imprisonment; in others, deportation, exile, or internment. In still others, the excluded may be put to death or kept in a state of slavery . . ."

Dr. Glynn's voice is high and clear, and he has the certainty of one who has been at the top of his profession for many years, accustomed to address the most prestigious academic gatherings. Even though he was speaking to a woebegone band of doomed and desperate outcasts on a windswept peak in southwestern Colorado, he retained his classroom manner. "One is led to the conclusion that, as civilization and exclusion are historically inseparable, there may be an inevitable and causal link between them," he said, as the wolves bayed downhill and our dogs lay crunching wildcat bones by the campfire. "A 'necessitous bond,' as my colleague Waldo Bailey has called it . . ." We listened in the heavy silence of fatigue. The relevance of Dr. Glynn's disquisition to our present problems seemed remote. I thought of the day to come. We would have to send a fishing party down to the stream. We were short of water and firewood. Would Seligson die? Dr. Zenger is behaving strangely—muttering to himself and digging in the ground to bury tufts of hair he pulled from his beard. Even Dr. Glynn is showing the strain. This must be the fifth time he has delivered this same lecture.

"Exclusion functions as a defining force," Dr. Glynn continued. "Its existence marks the boundaries of society, illuminating that society's values by its negative light. We know what we are by knowing what we are not. If there were no night, what would be the definition of day? What would be 'up' without 'down'? 'Black' without 'white'? How would free citizens realize the worth of their privileges and pleasures, if there were no identifying structure of denial . . . ?"

I couldn't help dozing—dozing and waking and dozing again, stung awake by the chill blasts of the mountain wind and the fear that dwells in me as in us all, then slumping back into an uneasy nodding sleep, hearing Dr. Glynn's voice in bits and pieces, as if the wind and my drowsiness had blown holes in it.

"...exclusion is the darkness that surrounds the comforting fire, it is the Wall that suffers the pounding of the sea so that the inland farms and cities may flourish, it is the evil that gives meaning to the good..." I glanced at my companions, their windburnt faces stunned with an animal exhaustion, solitary human lumps wrapped in skins and rags. Were they evil? Was their exclusion a historical necessity? "...the great fundamental myth of humanity—the story of the Creation—is based on exclusion, however it may differ among the various creeds," Dr. Glynn was saying. "Satan was cast out of Paradise, and Adam and Eve were banished from Eden (to cite the Christian version). What are these if not celebrations of the vital role exclusion plays in life? The existence of Heaven is predicated on the existence of Hell, the one being unimaginable without the other..."

The wind bit deeper. The fire was burning low. I could hear Dr. Zenger chuckling to himself. Ferguson lay snoring beside his ursid, one arm flung protectively across it. "...thesis and antithesis," said Dr. Glynn. "Christ and anti-Christ. Yin and yang..."

I spoke out: "But is it fair? This system—exclusion—is it fair?" Dr. Glynn turned his head my way, puzzled, as if he had heard but could not understand. Maybe he thought it was the wind making the fire crackle. I got to my feet, my eyes watering in the cold, and said it again, louder. "But is it fair, Dr. Glynn? Tell me that!" He paused then, regarding me with an uncertain expression.

"Fair?" he said, squinting at me, his face seeming youthful in that smoky light, like that of a wizened boy. "Of course it isn't fair, Fowke. Who said anything about its being fair? I said it was necessary; weren't you listening? We are necessary people! If it weren't for us, they couldn't exist; didn't you grasp that point?"

It was near midnight. The guards change then. I could tell because the dogs were stirring. They stand guard shifts, too, and with their uncanny sense of time, always let us know when a change is due. Dr. Glynn hadn't stopped talking. "We are at the outposts of civilization," he said, his voice rising squeakily in the wind. "Ours is a high and noble fate, ours is a destiny which . . ."

I didn't listen any more. I had to go on guard. It was Dr. Zenger's turn, but he is unreliable now, and we do extra duty to fill his place. I tramped some fifty meters north to a knoll where Cady was waiting to be relieved. She scrambled down, and I climbed up there, taking the full blast of the wind. My dog trotted back and forth on the ground below. When I turned to look back at the camp, I could see the long the long lean figure of Dr. Glynn still standing with his bony arms waving as he spoke on and on to the sleeping fugitives around the fire.

APRIL 26

I seem to be something of an oddity in this group. I am the only one who asks questions or who tries to figure out new ways of doing things. As a matter of fact, I am the only one who takes any initiative. (Ferguson has plenty of energy, but he is obsessed with his ursid carcass and fiddles with it to the exclusion of everything else.)

The others don't seem to welcome my efforts. I have the feeling they think I am pushy, even when they benefit by my ideas—for example, a double-net method for fishing, which has increased our catch.

I have repeatedly urged Dr. Glynn to make plans for getting out of these mountains for good, telling him that if we manage to survive the rest of the winter—and it is still winter up here, at least at night—we should try to work our way south and cross the border into Mexico. It is not an inviting prospect—hundreds of kilometers of rough and dangerous country, with ursids tracking us at every step and the border itself possibly guarded by an electrovallum—but our situation is desperate, and no one has suggested anything better. No one has suggested anything at all. Dr. Glynn has more or less agreed with me, but it is clear that the leadership of this trek will fall on me.

APRIL 29

Deprived of the Juvenor, we are decaying physically at a fearful rate, the way people did up until one hundred years ago—"aging naturally," I've heard it called, although it seems unnatural to me. Most of us are in the full vigor of adulthood—or should be— but we are crumbling and cracking now. Our faces are seamed and wrinkled, our hair is graying, our skin is rough and spotted, our bones ache, and our muscles strain over the simplest tasks. We don't have a mirror. I can't look at my image directly, but I can see what it must be in the faces around me. Our exclusion has condemned us to a premature death.

I've thought a lot lately of heading for Mexico alone. I could travel fast. I wouldn't have to be concerned about the others.

Julia might be down there now, waiting for me in Ojinaga. Or if she had to leave, she'd leave a message for me, and we'd be in touch again, instead of being cut off the way we are, lost to each other.

I think about that, and I think about her—about the color of her eyes, which are light the way the noon sky is light—pale and clear and strong—a blue that can deepen without darkening, changing as her mood changes.

I should have left Dr. Glynn and the others long ago. Except, without me, what chance would they have?

And I realize that I am a real excluded now, because my behavior is so powerfully swayed by primitive instincts, the aboriginal roots which my conditioning smothered but could not eradicate. I am torn between loyalty to the human group I happen to live with and a longing for one particular person, emotions I was taught to despise.

And yet I feel them.

I have told the others my story—the Wall, my exclusion, my escape—but they haven't told me theirs. Not one of them has. I know you aren't supposed to make personal confidences—it is an invitation to a more than casual interpersonal relationship—but we aren't living in society now, we are out here in the wilds, and some rules don't make sense any longer.

I've said this to my companions—and they haven't liked it, but what do they expect? Are they waiting for an amnesty? Do they think they'll be welcomed back in some day?

They remind me how I was in the early days of my exclusion. I couldn't accept it; I couldn't bear to think of myself as an excluded. I kept telling myself I hadn't changed . . . but after a while I had to face up to reality.

Why don't they?

The only one who has said anything about himself, apart from minimal career information, is Dr. Zenger. After the ursid attack, when he was treating my cuts, he told me he had chosen exclusion—and he gave a despairing sort of giggle. When I asked him why he'd done it, he just giggled again. Looking back at it, I can see that this was an early sign of his breakdown.

MAY 1

I have urged Dr. Glynn to move the camp down to the plateau. It would be warmer there; fishing and hunting would be better, too. I offered to carry Seligson down on my back. The old man didn't say yes or no, he said he'd think about it, but I have the feeling that he is too worn down to make any decision. The rest of them aren't any better. They sit around gloomy and lethargic between chores. Sometimes the dogs get playful, but nobody except me will play with them. I throw sticks for them to chase, and I pick off their tricks and burrs; I pat them and scratch their ears.

I am getting restless. Inactivity gets on my nerves. I have taken to going off by myself into the woods with a couple of dogs for company. Frankly, I prefer their society.

MAY 3

A strange episode, embarrassing in some ways. It may have a permanent influence on my relations with the members of Dr. Glynn's band.

Night before last I happened to lie down next to Dr. Raffy when I returned from guard duty. (I say "happened," but maybe it wasn't by chance.) A cold wind was blowing. I couldn't keep it from leaking in under my pelts no matter which way I turned. Dr. Raffy was within arm's reach, and without thinking what I was doing, I touched her shoulder. "I'm cold," I whispered. She was turned away from me and didn't respond, but I knew I had wakened her—I could sense her awareness, a sort of stiffening. I edged closer. "Aren't you cold?" I said. I was thinking how warm we'd be together and that there was no harm in it, without realizing the seriousness of what I was heading for. It was the wind that pushed me on, the wind that still had frost in it, and all the winds that had gone before, and the fear of ursids and death, and the yearning for a comforter when there was no comforter any more for me, and so it was a natural and simple impulse that made me reach out for the closest warmth there was.

I kept whispering to her about the cold and the wind as I inched her way, pulling my coverings along with me. I got one foot in, then a leg, then an arm, and as I felt the heat of her body, I was drawn in all the way until we were bundled there together. She seemed to vibrate, as if a part of her were resisting me and another part accepting me—desiring my warmth as I desired hers—and now and then she'd give a choked gasp, and she'd alternate between relaxing and even thrusting herself back against me and then going stiff again and trying to pull away. I didn't force her. I kept from putting my arms around her, as I wanted to do. I just lay there against her, warm as I hadn't been warm for months, a bone-deep warmth stirred by long slow surges of eroticism, and I could tell she was responding the same way, for her tensity diminished, her breathing came deep and regular, and she let herself go soft against me.

This led to something else. She happened to change position, turning over to face me, and we began to touch, with our fingers first and then with our mouths, and I find it hard to set down what happened even in the privacy of my micropen, partly out of modesty and a certain shame—I mean shame after the fact, because I didn't feel shame at the time. Something broke loose in us, something uncontrollable. It was like falling or drowning, where you struggle but can't help yourself; you are out of your element, and there is no stopping it. It was totally different from the stimulator, which is all pleasure, whereas this was violent and sweaty and awesome in the sense we knew we were shattering an absolute taboo, and it was as if we were possessed by demons.

We are both big and we must have made noise, and I'm sure we woke some of the other people. A dog got up and came over to us, putting its nose against my neck.

Looking back on this experience in flesh-contact sex, I can say that from the standpoint of sheer bodily gratification, it was better than nothing, but it demonstrated the limitations of the method. If I had to guess, I'd say we didn't get beyond the equivalent of Level 2 on the settings, hardly more than a heavy rubdown. Of course, you have to remember it was the first time, and it stands to reason that with practice, and under more relaxing circumstances, we'd be bound to get more out of it. As it was, we did feel a physiological peace when we'd finished, and we eased apart and slept the rest of the night.

The next thing I remember it was morning. Someone was feeding the fire. The dogs were stirring and shaking themselves. The new day was reddening the sky. Dr. Raffy scrambled out from under our mixed pelts, tying her clothes together, and hurried off toward the sanitary pits. She didn't come back for quite a while. I lay drowsing in the heat she'd left behind, and only after I finally got up, too, did I realize that the others were avoiding me, neither looking at me nor speaking to me, even when I said something that required a reply. Everyone seemed upset and shocked. Only the dogs came wagging up to me as usual.

My reactions were mixed. I realized I'd done something I

wouldn't have dream of doing if we'd been in anything resembling normal living conditions, but I felt that it was excusable under the circumstances, and besides, she'd accepted it, hadn't she? My feelings weren't eased when Raffy came back into camp, cast me a horrified glance, and stayed as far away from me as possible all day. As did the others.

At dusk I took the first turn of night guard duty; my post was a heap of rocks beyond the northern edge of the camp. After I'd been up there a few minutes, I saw Dr. Glynn clambering up to where I was. "Fowke," he said, and his voice was hoarse and shaky, perhaps because of his climb, "I hope I don't have to tell you that what you did was regressive and deplorable—a transgression of the fundamental values of civilized—"

"I was cold, Dr. Glynn."

"Cold? Cold? We're all cold, Fowke! But we can't permit ourselves to—to fall into savage and primitive—into practices that threaten the very—the decencies of our way of life . . ." He went on like that for a while, stammering and spluttering and repeating himself in his outrage.

"I'm sorry you're so upset by it," I said finally, "but I'm not going to apologize. My advice to you is to forget about it. We've got other things to worry about out here."

"My God, Fowke. Don't you see? We're living on the brink of a gulf here. We are caught between the ursids and our own incipient animalism. Which is the more terrible? Is physical death worse than moral death? If we allow all that is low and base in us to break loose, what will become of us? What hope can there be? Dr. Glynn was exclaiming into the wind, his skinny arms flapping in despair. "For the sake of the rest of us, you must promise me never to attempt such a despicable act again. Otherwise I cannot answer for the consequences. Flesh contact! I never thought I'd have to face such barbarism!"

In his agitation, he swayed and lost his footing and would have toppled off the rocks if I hadn't grabbed his arm to steady him.

"Don't touch me!" he cried out, jerking back.

"You'll fall, Dr. Glynn."

"I'd rather fall!"

"Don't be such a fool!" I hauled him around to a safer position before I let go.

He gave me a defiant glare and then descended to the ground.

"You haven't heard the last of this, Fowke! And to think I trusted your judgment!"

MAY 7

I thought this would blow over in a day or two. It hasn't.

The others still keep away from me. Every effort I've made to approach them—speak to them—has been rebuffed. Not even Ferguson will respond. I sleep apart, eat apart. They don't call me for guard duty. I do my turns anyway. When I volunteer to check the traps, there is silence. Nobody wants to go with me.

I set out alone again yesterday, crossing the stream where the rocks make steps and going into the woods to look at the nearest trap—and saw that something had beaten me to it. What had been a hare was nothing more than a few scraps of bloody fur. I went on toward the next trap and stopped dead in my tracks. A huge bear was feeding up there. It was enormous, had to be a grizzly, the first we'd seen. I ran back to give the warning—burst in out of breath, gasping out the news, which should have galvanized the camp, because, as McPartland once said, a grizzly may attack if he's hungry or grouchy, and he can shake you out of a tree, and the only defense is fire.

They paid no attention to me. They pretended not to hear. It was as if I didn't exist. Nobody asked me how big the damned thing was or how far off it was, nothing. A few of them sneaked anxious looks in the direction I'd come from, that was all.

"You'd better get some torches ready," I said. I was standing there sweating and angry, my fists clenched. "And you'd better lay some dry branches out around the perimeter to light in case he comes nosing close." They ignored me. It was incredible, stupid and infuriating. If someone else had given the alarm, they'd be taking the necessary precautions, all right—I could tell they were worried—but with me, it was as though they felt they'd be accepting me back if they let me know they'd heard me, and their feeling against me was stronger than their fear. I began yelling at them, stamping back and forth through the camp. "Are you people crazy? There's a real danger out there! Go out and take a look yourselves if you don't believe me!"

They didn't move. Didn't look at me. I went off and made my own torch, tied a bundle of twigs around the end of a branch, wrapping it with a dry rabbit skin, and took my place at the far end of the camp, with the dogs.

MAY 8

The grizzly hasn't approached us. He may have been satisfied with robbing our traps and gone on his way.

This is the sixth day of my ostracism.

MAY 10

By this time, planning ought to be well advanced for the move out of the mountains toward the south, but nothing has been done, and I have the feeling that nothing will be done.

These people have had two men killed (three, if you count Wright) and another one driven out of his senses and one so badly hurt he will be crippled for weeks...and they act as if I am their only problem.

MAY 13

I decided to approach Dr. Glynn and insist on discussing this idiotic and pointless situation, so last night, when he was on guard, I went out to the rocks and confronted him, knowing he couldn't walk away from his post.

"Dr. Glynn, we've got to talk about my position here. Things can't go on like this."

He turned frostily away from me and folded his arms.

"This is childish, Dr. Glynn. We're in danger here. We can't afford to waste time on petty squabbling."

"I don't speak to excluded," he said haughtily.

"Good God, we're *all* excluded here!"

"That's a matter of opinion," he replied. "My case is a special one. I have never accepted the judgment of the court, and I never will!"

"What difference does it make now, Dr. Glynn? We've got to organize ourselves to get down to the border. That's the important thing."

"For you, perhaps. I have no doubt that you were properly condemned—but I was not! The errors of my trial are bound to be rectified soon. I am certain that my colleagues are working night and day in my behalf. At any moment the pardon may be delivered."

I despaired in the face of this obstinacy. "Maybe you're right, Dr. Glynn," I said, to humor him. "But what about the others?"

"The others? Don't talk to me about others, Fowke!" He paced to the far edge of the rock, then back again, fuming. "What do I care about others? It's *my* case that matters!" He paced off again and stood with his back to me, his head flung back as though he were speaking to the stars. "I have nothing to hide—nothing! Let the record be examined! My documents are in perfect order—nothing is missing! My degrees, my commendations and awards! Citations from learned societies! Honors and tributes from throughout the civilized world!" Exclaiming and gesticulating, he turned to face me again, but he didn't seem to be looking at me. He was addressing shadows in his past.

"What weight can a youthful act of folly have against a lifetime of service, merit and duty? Is a man to be hounded to his grave for one minor transgression? A transgression at least in part justified by a social stigma for which he bears not the slightest responsibility?" Dr. Glynn paced about, casting defiant glances into the dark, as though an unseen tribunal were gathered there to hear his case. "Prejudice and spite, gentlemen. These are my enemies. *They* should be in the dock, not I. Very well, I am of viviparous origin. Is that a crime? Was it my fault? True, the actual charge was that I suppressed and concealed this fact—and I was wrong to it, freely admit—but I was a mere stripling at the time, gentlemen, an eager and ambitious youth who surrendered to a momentary impulse to remove an unfair disadvantage, for as we all know, my friends, viviparous citizens are discriminated against. 'A vip gets zip,' the saying is. But to have that jejune error rise up out of the files sixty years later to strike down a brilliant scholar—to drag his honored name through the dirt—gentlemen, such a gross miscarriage of justice must and will be expunged . . . !"

It was hopeless. I turned away and left the old man shouting into the night wind.

MAY 14

The situation is worse, if anything. They are whispering together. I think they are making their minds up about what to do with me.

I have the feeling that something ludicrous is about to happen . . . a monstrous irony.

I will be excluded by the excluded.

And I don't think I'm going to wait for that.

MAY 15

I left at dawn yesterday, when everyone was asleep except Ferguson at the lookout point. I raised my hand in a salute when I passed him. He must have known I wasn't coming back—I had my pelts wrapped and tied and slung over my shoulder—and he stole a look around, as if to be sure nobody was up who might see him do it, and then he gave me a half-hearted wave in return.

The shaggy mongrel we call Royal came trotting along with me. I was still angry at the way I'd been treated, and I was tempted to keep him for myself. Then I thought better of it. There are only three dogs now. Without me, Dr. Glynn and the others will need all the help they can get. So I ordered Royal back and went on alone.

I am heading west. In a couple of days I ought to be in Utah, and in a few more I should strike the Colorado River. I have in mind building another raft (a better one this time) to drift toward Mexico. I doubt that Julia will be there. She almost certainly has had to return to the U.S. by now—but who knows? She could be waiting for me. That thought gives me energy.

At least now I am better fitted for survival than I was when I left Kansas. I am tougher and more alert. The only thing that could kill me would be a grizzly—or an ursid. I am plagued by the feeling that one is tracking me, just out of sight. At dusk if I happen to see a solitary tree or a cactus in the distance, my heart gives a jump. At night I climb a tree and wedge myself in a fork of the branches—but the trees are thinning now. Soon I will be out in the open range.

MAY 18

The land is drier and rockier. I crossed two overgrown roads yesterday. Saw the ruins of a ranch. Since then, nothing. No trails, no signs that humans have ever passed this way.

The sky is enormous. The winds whip up veils of dust reddened by the sun. Lizards scatter among the rocks. There are vultures riding the high heat currents.

MAY 19

I am in the desert now, and it has nothing in common with what I remember from my tourist days, although the setting is the same. What a fool I was to think I had found solitude. No man is alone who can call a rescue hover whenever he wants. I had imagined that I was some solitary nomad experiencing primeval sensations of isolation, lost in the infinite eye of God—but I knew I had civilization a button-punch away.

The real Desert Experience is what I have now. It is true solitude, and solitude is fear.

MAY 21

Yesterday morning at about ten o'clock, to judge by the sun, I was walking through a dry ravine searching for snakes, now my chief source of food—I pin them down with a forked stick and then kill them with my club—when I sensed the presence of some large creature nearby. I can't explain exactly how I knew, for there was no sound in that desert quiet, not even the scrabble of a lizard or the sandpaper glide of a rattler. I was far from grizzly country. No cougars or wild goats would come here. It wasn't a fox—I had the clear impression of dimensions far larger than that. Besides, I would not fear a fox, and I was afraid. There was only one thing it could be, something which would have tracked me at a distance for days, remaining out of sight, slowly closing in.

I stepped into the shadow of a rock. There was no escape for me. I would either be captured, and perhaps maimed in the process, or torn apart on the spot. I could neither run nor hide nor fight.

I listened. I thought I could hear something now. Steps—and this was unusual, for they move without noise. I stared intently in that direction, holding my breath. For a moment, I wondered if what I was hearing was my own heartbeat, but no, they were steps—slow casual steps, a sort of lazy saunter. Whatever caused them was still around the bend of the ravine.

And then I heard the unmistakable sound of the breaking of wind—a fruity, full-blown trumpeting that echoed among the rocks.

Ursids do not fart.

I edged around the shelter of the rock.

It was a man. I remained motionless, watching him approach. He hadn't seen me yet.

He was a large, muscular, meaty man in shiny boots and whipcord pants and a yellow short-sleeved shirt, with a visored cap on his head. I would have known he was a tourist even if I hadn't seen the standard tourist lunch bag slung over one shoulder and the little communicator box he carried like a camera suspended from a strap around his neck. He had that glossy, well-fed look about him and a complacent smile of self-approval. He was indulging in the Desert Experience, he was bathed in the soul-expanding solitude the Tourist Board had guaranteed, he had an ample lunch in his bag, and he had just resoundingly liberated his guts of the pressure of gas.

It all happened quickly. Less than a minute. It seemed much longer.

The man saw me and stopped, looking at me with surprise. I must have presented a savage picture, gaunt and bearded, clothed in rough-cut animal skins knotted together by thongs, my skin darkened by dirt and smoke, pelts slung over my shoulder, my club in one hand. He wasn't alarmed. He was annoyed.

He planted his boots apart, put his hands on his hips, and stared at me, frowning. "This is a hell of a note," he grumbled to himself. Of course he recognized what I was, just as I had recognized him. I knew what he was thinking. I would have reacted in the same way myself, in his place. What was this hairy monstrosity doing, interrupting his solitude? The Tourist Board would certainly hear about this! In the meantime, what he was going to do with me? He could ignore me and go on his way, but that would violate the canon of good citizenship, not to mention the law that requires you to turn in excluded fugitives. But if he summoned a hover, he'd have to wait for its arrival, and if they didn't send an officer with the pilot, he might have to fly back to the base to keep me under guard. The whole day would be ruined! He glared at me in disgust, as if I had deliberately put myself in his way to cause him this unpleasantness.

We were less than twenty meters apart. I had begun approaching him, limping on the foot I'd bruised the day before. Maybe I had in mind making some appeal. What did it mean to him whether I was captured or not? To me, it meant everything. But I knew he had no mercy in him, no more than I had had once. He might have gone a step out of his way to avoid trampling a flower or crushing a beetle, but for a creature like me he would not swerve.

He reached for his communicator box. It was in a leather case. All he had to do was unsnap the top and then press the button.

We stood facing each other beneath the desert sky in the silence that had thickened, that engulfed us, heavy and suffocating. I saw him not only for what he was—a large and self-satisfied human animal in his prime, the product of decades of gratification—I saw him, too, as what I had been. A year ago I could have stood in his place, and if I had encountered a ragged fugitive in the desert, I would have regarded him as this fellow now regarded me, as something loathsome.

He would call the hover. I had to stop him. "Wait," I called to him, croaking the words in my dry, dusty voice, unused to speech. "Don't do that."

He didn't respond. I had less importance for him than a jackrabbit.

His hand reached the top of the leather box.

The revulsion I saw in his eyes I reflected now toward him. It was this that exploded in me.

His fingers opened the snap.

I hurled the club.

I had made it in my first days in Colorado out of a stout sapling, green and limber. Into one end I had wedged a sharp-edged stone that was pointed like a spearhead, lashing it tight with wet thongs that tightened as they dried. It was well-balanced and true in flight. I'd practiced my throw every day.

It hit him square in the middle of the forehead. He fell full-length, flat on his back.

I walked up to him. The blow had split his skull, the point driving into his brain. I could tell he was dead.

I removed the communicator box from around his neck and closed the snap.

Then I opened his lunch bag and wolfed down its contents: two sandwiches, a salad, a fruit pie, and a container of cold tea.

Afterward, I examined him. No heartbeat, no sign of breathing. He lay staring open-eyed into the blinding sun.

I stripped him of everything he wore: clothing, wristwatch, the identification bracelet on his right wrist, the silver ring on his left index finger. The body I dragged out of sight among a clutter of boulders. Vultures, insects and the sun would make short work of all but the bones.

At that point I had no clear idea of what to do. I remember thinking I should bury the clothing or burn it, except for the boots, which I needed, and the watch, which would be useful. I found his map and trail-locator in a side pocket of the lunch bag and realized that I could go to the trail lodge without risk. His travel slip showed he had it to himself until tomorrow at noon, when the hover would show up for him. I could ransack the place for food and clothes.

I folded his clothing inside my pelts, shouldered the bundle, and set off, the locator in my hand. It gave me a directional signal, homing in on pulsors set in the lodge walls.

It took me less than an hour to reach the place, a dome-roofed wooden cabin on a little rise, with a terrace in front where the hovers land to bring tourists and take them away again. The door lock was activated by the locator-beam, just as I remembered from my own Desert Experience.

The cabin was simply furnished: a bed, a table and a chair, a bathroom, a kitchenette, a stimulator, and to my surprise, something that hadn't been included in the lodges I had used: a Juvenor.

I could not recognize the man I saw in the full-length bathroom mirror. My filthy, matted hair was streaked with gray, as was my beard. My face was sharp and fierce, skin drawn tight over protruding facial bones, harsh deep lines cut beside the mouth and across the forehead. The eyes of this wild stranger had a feral gleam. His body coverings (you couldn't call them clothes), torn from various animals, formed a shapeless, stinking quilt, bound at the waist and legs with thongs and twisted vines.

I took a long, soaking shower, trimmed my beard close with some scissors and shaved the stubble. I was desperately tired but didn't dare sleep, for I knew I had to leave as soon as I could, and put the greatest possible distance between me and the search parties that would be dispatched the next day, when the tourist didn't appear for his hover return. I took the blankets off the bed and spread them on the floor and began laying out on them whatever I found that seemed worth taking.

The tourist's overnight bag contained a change of clothes, a pocket Librex and his documents, which I examined. He was named Dom Bastide and lived in Denver, where he was a Civserv Three—a middle-grade bureaucrat, deputy director of a minor agency in the Commerce Department.

I was ready to leave, but I couldn't bear the thought of going without a ten-minute turn in the Juvenor. (The stimulator I couldn't use, as this would put my TE readings on the open scan.) I entered the capsule, set the timer so I wouldn't fall asleep, and emerged refreshed and vigorous. A glance in the mirror showed that even this brief treatment had produced a visible benefit, freshening my skin, smoothing out some lines, and giving a gloss to my hair.

His boots fit me. The whipcord pants would have fit, too, before the wilderness stripped me down to skin and bone; they were baggy in the thighs and slack around the waist. The yellow shirt was loose on me as well, but the light twill jacket he'd hung on a hook by the bed sat well on my shoulders. My old skins I decided to bury outside, under a bush; the pelts I would carry for extra covering.

It was when I took another look in the mirror that the idea struck me.

If Bastide appeared for the hover flight as scheduled, there would be no search. He would not be missing.

I didn't resemble him, except in height—but who would know the difference? Not the felid pilot of the hover. And not the TR staff at the resort center at Blanding, where his travel slip showed he had a room reserved. The only risk was that some other tourist there would know the man—but that seemed extremely unlikely. People take their vacations alone. Whoever knew him would be back in Denver, and there wouldn't be many of them—his co-workers at the office and two or three persons who lived in the same apartment building.

I cut my hair short with the scissors. Not a professional job, but it will have to do. I will keep the cap on my head, pulled low. My face is another matter. Even shaven and clean and dressed in Bastide's clothes, I look like what I am. I had better wear his dark glasses.

MAY 22

I am back in the modern world.

The hover arrived at noon today on schedule. The felid didn't even glance at me when I got in.

In twenty minutes we had landed at Blanding, a small desert resort with a central services building surrounded by individual cottages.

I checked into my cottage—Bastide's cottage—and had a murid barber sent over to give me a proper haircut. After that I ordered and ate two complete meals, not so much from hunger as to start filling out my frame.

I had to kill Bastide. I had no choice. I feel no guilt, no remorse, not even regret. Murder does not exist. (I think this is legally true. It is so rare that it has been dropped from the list of punishable offenses.) There are no crimes of passion. (There are no passions.) Death does not exist, either. You don't see it; you never hear of it. When an aged person begins to fail, he or she is taken away somewhere (to a rest home, I suppose), simply disappearing from the world, with no goodbyes, no remembrance, nothing. Life is stimulation. When life ends, stimulation ends; that is all. Mourning, grief, guilt—these emotions belong to the past. We feel them no longer. If I were fool enough to try to explain what I did—murdered a man—to the fellow in the next cottage, he wouldn't understand me. He would have no comprehension of the state of mind I was in at the time, he would be unable to conceive of an emotion strong enough to lead to such an act. He wouldn't be horrified, he'd be puzzled or simply wouldn't believe me.

There is no murder, there is no death. But I still think sometimes about the man I killed, his body ripped by vultures, gnawed
by foxes, his bones bleaching in the sun.

This afternoon I ran through the Vidipix recall to pick up back
news about the Wall. There wasn't any. Not a single item since
October, when my exclusion began.

I tried an assortment of topics, working the recall for a couple
of hours, and came up with three suggestive stories: a sharp
decline in farm production in East Carolina, ascribed by the Department of Agriculture to "unseasonable meteorological factors,"
severe February storms in north-central Florida, damaging citrus
crops and forcing the evacuation of several localities (not identified), and the "temporary closing" of the Hatteras Complex for
repair and renovation of tourist facilities.

I put in a telemin call to the Neptune city hall—and got a recorded
message saying that the number was out of order.

Same response from South Poseidon.

I tried to make a reservation for an East Coast satellite skyride
and was informed that seats were oversold. No more bookings
were being accepted. For how long, they couldn't say.

Something has happened, something on a vast and terrible
scale—and the news is being suppressed or distorted. This is clear
to me now beyond any doubt.

What do I do next? The prudent thing would be to follow Bastide's schedule—two more days out here—and then go to Denver
on his return ticket and try to arrange a flight to Mexico from
there. It might seem strange for a tourist to abandon his vacation
so abruptly; I want, above all, to avoid drawing notice.

Once I've made my arrangements, I can get a message to Julia
via VX.

MAY 23

Bastide's schedule called for him to attend a program of Indian ceremonial dances this morning, so I thought I'd better go with the other tourists, some twenty of them. We were driven across the desert and up to the top of a plateau where the dancers were waiting for us with their drums and feathers and bracelets—all TRs, cleverly costumed to resemble actual Indians. From where we sat, you couldn't tell the difference.

According to the program, the dances have been reproduced with painstaking historical accuracy by a team of TR design engineers under the direction of Dr. Norman Kearney of the University of Utah. The real Indians who used to perform these ceremonies have long since been genetically and socially absorbed into society at large—I suppose I have some in me—and, as far as I know, there aren't any pure-bloods left. Their traditions, however, have been preserved through the work of Dr. Kearney and other scholars, so we are assured that nothing essential has been lost.

I have been expecting arrest at any moment since I arrived here, but only today have I realized how safe I am. The other tourists represent no threat. Nobody has shown any curiosity in me; no one has given me more than a passing glance, no one has said a word to me. There is no idle talk among strangers, no casual remarks, no polite social smiles. Each person acts as if others simply don't exist. It is a social attitude that grows on us like a shell; nothing can shatter it.

I had forgotten how strong it was.

There is only one person here who is constantly aware of the others, and that is me. I am the one who keeps searching faces, looking for danger signs. That's the instinct of my weeks in the wilderness, where survival depended on an awareness of each patch of sunlight, every sound. It is different here. Survival depends on *un*awareness now. I must behave like these people, must resemble them, must get that glaze on my face that means others do not exist. I must learn to exclude them.

MAY 24

Two outings this morning. First we were taken to Lake Powell to watch the water-sculpture display; underwater machines produce jets which create spectacular images, subtly colored by special dyes. The show we saw told the story of the winning of the West. We saw the pioneers and their wagons, battles with the Indians—giant water-figures of men and horses galloping through the reddened mists of battle—and the cowboys with their endless herds. It was a marvel of artistic engineering, and we all applauded, but it was boring, to tell the truth. It had no real meaning for us—not that people don't know about those events of the past, it's that none of it touches us emotionally. It isn't supposed to. Nothing is. You sit there watching, the way you watch the Vidipix. It is something to do.

From there we travelled to one of the Bryce Canyon archaeological digs, where specially fabricated TRs work under the direction of Professors Hoagland and McCabe of Harvard West. The TRs are mole-sized and burrow through the sandy soil, seeking artifacts. There are hundreds of them at work, hidden beneath the surface, which ripples and heaves like a lake agitated by the wind.

This afternoon we are to visit a longevity research center south of here.

MAY 25

What happened yesterday has shaken me badly. I couldn't sleep last night.

After lunch we were hovered to the longevity center, several low rectangular buildings edged by green lawns and tended by murid gardeners. This complex was surrounded by a high electric fence; beyond that, desert.

An information officer guided us through the labs, where human and felid researchers worked amid a maze of complicated gadgetry, and presented us to the director—a geriatrician named Bayliss Dean—who explained various facets of the center's work, aided by charts and graphs; senior staff members were called in to elucidate particular points.

The aim of the program is to discover ways of retarding the aging process or even reversing it—"our dream of dreams," Dr. Dean said to us—using implants, biothermy, chemisorbents, etc.

We were led about the place for nearly an hour, visiting staff offices and quarters, the communications center, storage and maintenance areas, and I don't know what else. Whatever interest I might have had in this program was overshadowed by my constant worry about exposure. It may have been my imagination, but every time we passed a security point, the ursid on duty seemed to bristle. I stayed in the middle of the group.

Every now and then we would see a patient in a hospital gown being pushed along in a wheelchair. Once someone was trundled past on a wheeled stretcher. I asked if the center had a hospital for the treatment of aged citizens. "We provide all curative services," the information officer replied, "using the latest methods and techniques." I took a close look at the next patient we encountered—a pale fellow with anxious eyes two orderlies were wheeling along the corridor—and he didn't seem very old to me.

We took a stroll outside to admire the gardens and the desert view, with the Abajo Mountains along the horizon, and I noticed at some distance from the rest of the complex a building we hadn't visited. The information officer didn't offer to take us there. Instead he led us back inside and up a flight of stairs. We emerged in an amphitheater whose tiers of seats overlooked an operating area where white-robed doctors and nurses were busy around a pair of long tables, surrounded by the usual paraphernalia of machines and tubes and monitors.

"This is the heart of the longevity center," the information officer said with pride. "Here is the final testing ground of orthopedic theory and analysis—the staging area of the future of civilized humankind." He went on in this vein, speaking in reverently lowered tones, as we peered down at the surgeons bending over the tables.

"What are they working on?" I asked our guide. "Are those laboratory animals?"

"You might call them that," the man replied. "Naturally we use experimental subjects which are as close as possible to ourselves."

I couldn't see much of these creatures, hidden as they were by the operating teams, no more than a limb here and there, swathed in surgical sheets. "Are they using apes?" I asked.

My voice must have risen, for our guide politely indicated that I should maintain silence. At one of the tables, the surgeons and their assistants stepped back with the air of having concluded a difficult piece of work, and we all got a good view of the subject.

It wasn't an ape. It was a man. He lay with one leg uncovered—not a real leg, but an artificial one. I recognized it as the lower extensor of a large TR. "That's a man," I whispered to the information officer. "They've put an ursid leg on that man. What happened—was he in an accident? Did he lose his real leg?"

The officer didn't hear me; perhaps he chose not to respond. It was time to go. He beckoned the group to follow him back down the stairs and through a passageway to another room. "This is the post-operative recovery area," he said. "And just beyond you will see the physical therapy section."

Two patients lay in bed in the recovery area, tended by murid nurses. They were asleep or unconscious. We weren't allowed to linger there but were ushered into the therapy section. Here were exercise machines of various kinds. Several patients were using them, assisted by orderlies under the supervision of a physician. One man was equipped with an ursid upper extensor as an artificial arm and was clumsily trying to pick up small objects from a table with it; another was staggering around the room on a pair of lower extensors, which had replaced his legs, accompanied by an orderly ready to catch him if he fell.

Dr. Dean, the director, had come in and began telling us about the enormous progress the orthopedic surgeons were making in perfecting these prosthetic devices, adapting TR parts for human use. "The human limb loses strength and efficiency with age," he said, "but an extensor will last indefinitely, and its operation, electronically actuated, requires no expenditure of physical effort on the part of the subject. In theory, a man so equipped could run at top speed all day without working up so much as a drop of perspiration."

I spoke up: "Dr. Dean, where do these patients come from? Do you keep them in that building we didn't get to see? And who are they? Are they excluded?"

Dr. Dean gave me a long look, as did the information officer. I was the only tourist who had asked questions. The others had observed everything with the same dispassionate calm they had displayed at the Indian dances and the water spectacle.

"Our subjects," said Dr. Dean, "are willing volunteers. I regard them with admiration. To my mind, their courage and devotion more than make up for any deficiencies they may have with respect to social origin or civil status." He was regarding me narrowly, as if trying to penetrate my sun glasses. The other tourists had edged away from me and were casting me disapproving glances. I felt the chill of suspicion and resolved to say no more. To my relief, Dr. Dean's scrutiny was interrupted by a message on his call box, and with a final glance at me he excused himself and went on his way.

The information officer conducted us into another room in the physical therapy section. At a certain point he stopped us and placed one finger to his lips. In the center of the room, suspended from a rack that hung from the ceiling, was what appeared to be an ursid. Its upper extensors dangled limply at its sides; its lower ones barely touched the floor. The information man spoke to us in a whisper. "Here we are in the presence of an orthopedic masterpiece," he said. "Its significance for future geriatric research can hardly be overestimated. Kindly remain at this distance and refrain from any noise or sudden movement, since the subject is still in a recuperative stage and is easily alarmed by phenomena it cannot immediately identify."

I stared at the hanging figure and saw that it was not exactly an ursid—that is, not completely. It wore a short hospital gown, open halfway down the front; there seemed to be skin showing in the opening, pale white skin sparsely covered by whitish hair. The head casing, too, was not fully closed in the lower front; it revealed a mouth—a human mouth—with parted lips, above a chin that bristled with beard stubble. The body feebly swayed, as if disturbed by a breeze, although there was no breeze there.

All of a sudden a groan emerged from the mouth, a groan and then a sigh. One of the grabs twitched convulsively, snapping blindly in the air.

"Our presence has been detected," whispered the information officer. He renewed his warning signal for silence, with a special look in my direction. I needed no such reminder. I stood speechless before this thing—this half-ursid, half-man—struck by amazement and dread. Was it alive? Was there a functioning brain within that casing?

Now it was uttering other sounds—murmurs, gasps and what might have been mumbled words.

"I believe it's trying to communicate with us," whispered the information officer.

The figure shuddered, as if in pain. Its upper extensors jerked up, and the grabs joined across its midsection. It spoke: "My friends, I cannot see you clearly—my vision is not what it once was—but I know you are there, and I welcome you to—" It broke off with a gasp and then repeated what it had just said, word for word. Again it broke off, and again it returned to the beginning and repeated what it had said before.

The information officer shook his head with a rueful expression, as if in sympathy with the ursid-man and its halting efforts to speak to us. The creature had fallen silent, and its grabs disengaged themselves, flopping loosely to its sides once more. Our guide looked around at us and shrugged his shoulders. He turned on tiptoe and was about to lead us out again, when the voice resumed, more forcefully than before.

"Ladies and gentlemen, I am deeply gratified to have been summoned at last to resume my rightful place among you," it said, crisply enunciating each word. "Justice has triumphed at last! The grave wrong done to me has been righted—and I am happy to offer my humble services in this pioneering effort. I may be forgiven a certain presumption, I trust, if I say that I have united, in my own person, the forces of Science and Nature, as part of civilization's constant struggle to extend the frontiers of knowledge. As my former colleague Waldo Bailey once said, humankind advances across a field of fire. Each step may be agonizing, but a glorious destiny awaits us!"

With this, the voice ceased, and the jaws closed with an audible snap.

The information officer waited for a few moments, but the ursid-man gave no further signs of animation. It hung silent and immobile before us.

"I think it's finished now," the officer whispered, beckoning us to leave the room. He had to come back for me. I hadn't moved. I stood staring at the thing that dangled slackly from the ceiling rack.

I had recognized the voice. It was that of Dr. Glynn.

PART
SIX

MAY 26

It may have been at the Denver airport that they got a signal on me. Deplaning passengers file through a passageway before entering the terminal, and it could be that they have scanners there, including the kind that can identify you by body heat-pattern analysis.

I wasn't aware that there was anything wrong. I took a cab to Bastide's apartment and changed into clean clothes, putting on one of his lightweight suits. Just by chance I took a look out of the window and saw two police machines pull up on the street below.

Maybe they were there on other business. I didn't wait to find out.

I ran down the fire stairs to the basement and out the back way, through an alley to the next block, where I caught a surfaceway car to Capitol Center.

Since then I have been wandering in Denver—the museums, the public buildings, the parks. I spent the night in a public comforter, slept standing up, like a horse.

* * *

I could have been in Mexico by now. There was a flight to Mexico City that departed twenty minutes after my arrival. By the time they could have identified me by the scanner (if there was one) and linked me to Bastide, I'd have been across the border.

But I didn't go.

I have decided to return to the Wall and see what's happening there with my own eyes.

It won't be easy. They must be watching the airports and glassway stations, probably the wheel agencies, too, and I have to assume that departing tourist groups are scanned as well.

If they captured Dr. Glynn, they must have captured the others. Or killed them. If I'd stayed, I might be on one of those surgical tables myself, getting a new pair of legs in the interests of science and civilization.

I sent a VX to Julia at Atlantis North. ARRIVED DENVER. I signed it *T. O. Wall.*

I won't know whether she got it or not. She may have been posted somewhere else.

MAY 27

I keep trying to figure out a way to get out of Denver without being caught. I stay on the move, watching for security police. I feel safest among groups of tourists; I keep switching from one to another. In the past two days I have visited the Capitol three times and have toured the other public buildings twice at least. These structures are reproductions of the originals left behind in Washington, except that they are twice as big. The effect is stunning: all that white marble, those stupendous columns, the towering facades. The top of the Washington Monument is sometimes obscured by clouds. The ceremonial Marine guards in front of the White House are outsize, too—the biggest ursids I have ever seen, standing eight feet tall.

* * *

At the Library of Congress I riffled through a Librex listing of federal officials and discovered that Barney Dragomine had been appointed as Presidential Science Adviser in January. So he is here in Denver, in some office in the White House.

The moment I saw his name, the idea leaped into my mind—*find him, tell him about the Wall. Maybe he doesn't know, maybe he can do something,* but of course I realized that it would be insane to try such an impossible thing. I'd be stopped before I got anywhere near him—stopped and arrested, and then I'd disappear into a punishment camp that would make the one at the Hinge seem like a holiday.

Dragomine might as well be on the other side of the world as far as I am concerned.

MAY 28

I was riding the surfaceway on Pennsylvania Avenue this afternoon when three security agents got on at the Justice stop to check identifications. We all had to get our cards out and have them ready. The car was crowded, and I was able to jostle a man and knock his card from his hand. I stooped and picked it up, but handed him mine instead. He didn't notice the switch. The agents took one glance at Bastide's card and hauled the fellow away. I knew it wouldn't be long before they discovered the mistake, so I got off at the next stop. Within a few minutes, the streets were swarming with security machines, and uniformed TRs were stopping everybody, including tourist groups. The entire zone was being sealed off.

I entered the nearest office building and took the shoot to the roof. The moment I stepped out, I saw a hover beating up from the Capitol. Three others were coming from the north. I ducked inside and went down the fire stairs to the top floor to search for a refuge. I could hear noises below—footsteps and doors banging. I had to hurry. They'd be on my floor before long.

The first room I looked into was empty. The next was occupied by fixed felids working at long assembly tables. I couldn't go in there.

There were double doors at the end of the corridor. I opened them, slipped inside, and closed them behind me. The room was large and dim, and full of crates—huge ones, twice my height. I groped my way among them. The floor was dusty and littered with scraps of packing material; the air smelled stale. The windows were too high for me to reach; besides, they were covered by metal grates.

I could hear the patrol coming along the corridor outside and hurried around, searching for a hole to crawl into. I squeezed between the last two crates—and saw before me twenty or thirty ursids, their casings gleaming in the dusty light. Some were huge, like the Marine guards. Others were of the smaller standard sizes. They stood massed before me, ready to rush over me, tumble me down, crush me with their weight and force.

And then I realized they weren't ursids. Not yet. They were ursid shells, awaiting assembly.

The double doors burst open, and the lights flooded on. I took refuge among the ursid shells, working my way to the back. The casings were lightweight; I could shift them to allow my body to pass. I reached the wall and crouched there. Now I could hear the swift scrabble of a murid as it methodically searched the room. If it were a true hunting murid, it would detect me by heat and odor; even a simple tracker ought to pick up the trail I made in the dust.

But it didn't. At least I don't think it did. It came near enough— I could hear it pawing at the outer row of casings—but then it rushed off again, and in a few moments the lights were extinguished, and the doors slammed.

I can't be sure I'm out of danger. The murid might have sensed my presence and gone to summon help.

I have waited five minutes, counting the seconds.

Nothing has happened.

But how am I going to get out of here?

MAY 29

I don't know how the idea came to me, it may have been because I knew I was surrounded by TRs, TRs everywhere—the security cordon that sealed the zone, the dozens of murids hunting through the buildings (they'd be back where I was soon enough, to take a more thorough look), and even in my temporary refuge I was in the midst of them, the empty ursid shells looming over me. I was a lone trapped human submerged in this robot ocean. No way out. Couldn't run or hide, couldn't burrow, couldn't fly, couldn't make myself invisible...

It was the thought of invisibility that caught in my mind.

I laid out some of the shells, measuring their length and the size of the inner hollows where the KN-links would be installed. The Marine guard shells were too big, the ordinary patrol shells too small, but after removing all my clothes except for my shorts (to which I clipped the micropen), I managed to wedge myself into a police ursid casing. It wasn't sealed yet. I could separate it in the middle and put on the two halves one at a time. The parietal casing wasn't joined, either, and I worked it down over my head like a helmet.

The shell hadn't been built for a human frame, that was clear. My feet were painfully jammed into the podalic bases, and since ursids have no knees, I had to walk stiff-legged. Ursids have no buttocks either, and I was mightily squeezed there. If I'd been carrying my pre-exclusion weight, I could never have stuffed myself in. My straight-ahead vision through rivet holes in the parietal casing was adequate, but I couldn't look down, and in order to see to one side, I had to turn myself that way.

A more serious problem was the absence of grips. This would be noticed at once. I knew there must be scores of grips packed in one of the sealed crates, but I couldn't get at them. I had to have a substitute that would pass muster. I picked up Bastide's boots and held them by the soles, so that the uppers protruded from the extensor openings, and hoped they would be accepted as one of the special grip attachments with which ursids are equipped for particular tasks.

I practiced my movements, experiencing considerable discomfort. I had to walk with most of my weight on my toes, and I feared that this, combined with my inability to bend my knees, would touch off leg cramps. The thoracic casing was big enough, but the parietal's mandibular hinge pinched my chin, and the ventilation was poor. Perspiration rolled down my chest and legs. I could feel it gathering at my feet.

But it was the ursid shell or nothing.

I extracted myself to take a final rest, massaging my feet and calves to prepare them for the torture that lay ahead. Then I hid Bastide's clothes in a corner of the room, climbed into the casing, stalked to the doors, opened them, and entered the corridor.

The first test came on the fire stairs. A patrol ursid was standing on the landing between floors. I didn't have much leisure to worry about him, my concentration being focused on the steps, which were the devil to negotiate stiff-legged on my toes and without downward vision; with those damned boots in my hands, there was no way I could steady myself on the banister.

I sensed no movement from the ursid when I passed him, although in my imagination I felt his gaze boring into the back of my neck as I jerkily descended.

I likewise passed patrol TRs at other landings and in the ground-floor lobby. This was encouraging, but I was afraid that sooner or later I would get near one tracked for heat detection—provided I didn't stumble and fall flat or go into a screaming leg cramp first.

Ahead of me was the cordon—a line of police ursids posted along Pennsylvania Avenue at regular intervals, with human and felid officers standing in the shade of the trees on the other side, watching and waiting. In the distance I could see the giant dome of the Capitol; behind it rose the snowy summits of the Rockies.

I didn't hesitate. I stalked between the nearest pair of TRs and crossed the avenue, trying to simulate a special-mission ursid on a homing track. One of the officers seemed to eye my boot-top grips curiously, but that was all.

Sharp pains were cutting through my feet. My legs strained and ached. Sweat sluiced down my forehead and into my eyes, blurring my vision. Every step was an agony. I could not vary my pace or show uncertainty about direction. Ursids will veer around obstacles or hop low ones, and they will obey traffic signals at crossings, but otherwise they proceed with the regularity of clocks.

I had passed the cordon. Now what? Ursids don't board buses or planes, they don't rent machines. Even if I had the stamina to reach the outskirts of Denver and find a secluded spot where I could safely shed my shell—a clear impossibility, since I was already on the verge of collapse—I would be worse off than ever. I would emerge from my casing with nothing to wear but my shorts and the boots, and how far would I get like that?

The day was failing. The sun was ready to slide down behind the Rockies. I didn't know where I was. All I could think of was the next excruciating step. How to stay upright. How to keep from bumping into things: people, lampposts, murid messengers. I stalked ahead, half-blinded, my thoughts confused by fear and physical torment. I felt the pressure of the shell, the pain, the constriction, the desperation. I was obsessed by my need to obey the laws of the ursid. It was no longer my refuge but my prison. It clamped my legs, my throat, stabbed my feet; it was enclosing me, binding me, possessing me. Crossing another street, I saw an ursid coming toward me with heavy stilted steps, the low-hanging afternoon sun glinting off its metaled surface. It grew larger and more menacing as it advanced, heading directly at me— and only at the last moment did I realize what it was in time to veer away, otherwise I would have walked smack into the window of the store that had tricked me with my own reflection—the brother image of that half-man, half-ursid which had dangled from the rack at the longevity center—the shining carcass of the ursid Fowke.

It was evening, and I found myself in a park (I was so exhausted that I was in the middle of it before I realized what it was). It was neither large nor dark nor thickly provided with trees and shrubs, but my body was screaming for relief, and I flung myself

full-length into the nearest clump of bushes and slowly and painfully extracted my legs from the shell, and then my head and my
upper half, and lay there like a dead man. I slept until the cold
woke me during the night—and then I realized where I was.
Through the branches I could see the spotlighted facade that
loomed above the trees, dreamlike with its shining portico and
lofty columns.

And I knew I was in Lafayette Park, across from the White
House.

I fell back into a numbed trance of fatigue. Woke to sunlight and
fading dreams. Birds flashed in the trees. A squirrel sat studying
me as I lay naked under the bush. I could hear traffic along the
avenue. A clock tolled the hour. I lost count of the strokes. Was
it eight, nine? A cold film of perspiration broke across my back
and shoulders. I hurriedly pulled the upper half of the shell over
my head, put on the parietal casing, and worked my legs into the
extensor tubes.

I could feel the warmth of the sunlight through the light alloy
of my shell (and wondered if the rising heat later on might not
cook me inside like a lobster). I had no idea of where to go or
what to do—I wasn't thinking about Barney Dragomine then, at
least not consciously—but I found I was heading toward the
White House. It seemed to draw me like a magnet, and in my
dazed condition, I had the strange sensation that I wasn't so much
moving toward it as it was approaching me—the high ornamental
ironwork fence, the great double gate, the statuelike figures of
the Marine guards, the green sweep of the lawn—everything
appearing to bob and waver nearer with my every step.

The avenue shuttled beneath my feet. The giant guards jerked
closer. They didn't seem to register me. To them I was just an
ursid. The gates stood open. I entered. The driveway pulled spas-
modically beneath me as the portico swelled near, its white columns towering up. A felid, attired in a frock coat with brass
buttons, stood in the entranceway. Behind me came a group of
tourists. I must have been moving slowly, for they overtook me

before I reached the portico, and the surprise of finding myself
in the midst of these humans made me miss the raised curbing.
I stumbled and lurched against one man, which steadied me.
Otherwise I would have fallen. He recoiled and cast me an in-
dignant glance—and then another glance of curiosity and distaste
(he may have caught my odor, which by this time must have been
strong), but he did nothing, continuing with the group. I walked
in their wake through the portico and up the steps and inside.
The frock-coated felid squeaked at me, but of course I had no
idea what it meant, if it meant anything. I trailed behind the
tourists across the carpeting, past portraits and antique tables,
past uniformed TR guards with their extensors folded majestically
across their chests, past state rooms on display, their treasures
blocked off by velvet ropes. In a full-length mirror I saw myself—
and realized I had lost the boots; I must have left them back in
the park. The tips of my fingers protruded from the extensor
tubes. I withdrew them, doubling my fists, and turned the first
corner I came to, moving away from the tourists, and hurried
into a more modern section of the White House—a brightly
lighted corridor lined with offices. The first few human bureaucrats were arriving for work with leisurely steps. They paid no
heed to the sweating, stinking ursid stalking by. I turned another
corner, started along another corridor.

Now there was one thought in my mind: *find Dragomine.*

I glanced at the doors that I passed. Some had titles on them,
others were blank. I knew I had to find the right one soon. More
people were arriving for the workday. I was bound to be reported.

After the third turning of the corridor, I saw a door labeled
Scientific Advisory Commission. That was the one I wanted.

I entered the reception area of a suite of inside offices. The
staff hadn't arrived. The only employee there was the fixed communications felid, which sat at its terminal, its triple extensors
folded. I passed through to the inner office corridor. Dragomine's
name was on the door of the corner office, larger than the others.
I slipped inside. It was furnished with a large desk, sofa, table,
bar, comforter, etc., and a bathroom. I searched the place, hoping
he kept a change of clothes handy, but there was nothing to wear

except a pair of hand towels. My feet were in agony, so I stripped off the bottom part of the shell in the bathroom and hid there, listening at the door. In a little while, a felid secretary entered the office, turned on the lights, dusted the desk, activated Dragomine's scan with the overnight VXs, then went out. This was a positive sign. I'd been afraid this might be one of Dragomine's days off, but now I felt he would come.

Soon enough I heard footsteps. It had to be Dragomine. I opened the bathroom door a crack to get a look at him. He was a stout athletic-looking man in his seventies and moved with solemnity and confidence. He sat behind his desk and began examining the VXs, disposing of them with quick taps on the executor.

I was dazed with exhaustion and anxiety and wasn't sure what to do, except I knew I had to confront him, tell him about the Wall. Make him listen, make him understand. Convince him to tell the President and mobilize the government to take emergency measures. Save the Wall.

While I was wondering how to approach him, he turned in his chair and looked my way—he must have sensed my presence—and I had to move fast.

I came out of the bathroom, crossed the room, and closed the outer office door. He sat stock-still, amazed. "Please don't signal for assistance, Mr. Dragomine," I told him. He was staring at me in astonishment. "All I want is five minutes of your time," I said. Fearing that he would leap up and try to run past me, I picked up the nearest thing that resembled a weapon—a bronze statuette of Abraham McKay that stood on top of the Librex. "Don't be alarmed, sir," I said. "I don't intend to hurt you." He made a little choking sound but said nothing. "Let's go into the bathroom to talk," I said. "We can have some privacy there."

Dragomine remained in his chair, transfixed by the extraordinary hybrid which stood before him: an ursid with bare human legs, brandishing the image of the father of the Atlantic Rampart System.

"Let's go, Mr. Dragomine," I said. "Get up. I don't have much time."

He pushed back his chair and rose to his feet. "What do you want?" he asked, as I motioned him toward the bathroom. "Who are you? Is this some sort of joke?"

"It isn't a joke. It's about the Wall. You must know about what's happening there."

He edged back, wary of the statuette I held. It was hatchetlike in form, for McKay's arms were outstretched in a grandiose gesture, symbolizing the reach of his vision.

Once inside the bathroom, he retreated to the far wall. I worked my way out of the ursid's thoracic and parietal casings and stood before him naked, except for my shorts. My appearance as a human didn't seem to reassure him, and I didn't have to guess why; the wilderness had stamped a ferocious look on me.

"My name is Fowke, Mr. Dragomine. William Fowke. You don't know me, but I used to be engineering director at Baltimore Canyon before I was excluded."

He must have known I was an excluded, but when I spoke the word, he couldn't repress a grimace.

"Fowke?" he said. "I think I remember the name." He was watching me apprehensively. I don't suppose he'd ever seen an excluded in his life.

I knew I had to speak fast. Someone might come in at any minute—the secretary, a staff assistant—and Dragomine might yell for help. I told him everything I could remember, getting it mixed up in my haste: told him about the seepage at Baltimore Canyon, about Dr. Matthews's refusal to believe me, about the failure of the sensors to record what was happening, what I'd seen up at the Hinge, the rumor Dr. Grandgent had reported of disaster at East Georgia.

He listened to me worriedly, his gaze shifting between me and the door.

"So what's going on?" I said. "You must know about it. Are the rumors true? Why have they closed Hatteras? Why aren't they booking skyrides?"

Dragomine cleared his throat. "We're well aware of the situation at the Rampart System," he said.

"You do know about it, then."

"Certainly. And I can tell you that everything is taking place within the predicted range of norms, without significant variation."

"You mean there aren't any big problems?"

"No problems that weren't foreseen, Fowke. We haven't been taken by surprise."

"I don't understand. You mean that the Deeps have sealed at Baltimore Canyon? They've sealed everywhere?"

He gave an involuntary shudder, perhaps a delayed reaction of fear, and I realized that he'd probably never known fear before. "No problems," he repeated. "I can't say more than that."

"You've got to say," I told him harshly. "What about the Deeps?"

"The trouble with my trying to explain things to you is that you don't have the background," he said in an uneasy voice. "You don't have—you didn't have access to high-level security information, so inevitably you have seen things from the local administrative point of view—I would have myself, in your place—without being able to interpret their meaning as part of the general picture."

"What does that mean? Have the Deeps sealed or not?"

Dragomine hesitated. "I shouldn't say anything on this subject, Fowke. Even if you were still an employee of the System, it would be a violation of security." He gave me a quick glance. "In point of fact, the Deeps have a largely conceptual existence."

I frowned at him. "Conceptual—?"

"They were planned, and prototypes were installed in test zones during construction, but there were problems, serious problems—"

"What are you trying to tell me?"

"—problems which couldn't be resolved with the technology of the time, and so—" He broke off and shrugged.

"And so? And so what? What happened?"

"Nothing further was done."

"Nothing was done? Are you saying that there are no Deeps? That can't be true! The Deeps run beneath the entire System! It's a matter of historical record!"

"That's the official record, Fowke. National security considerations required the government to treat the question that way, in order to reassure the people."

I was starting to sweat. I couldn't believe what he was telling me. "Wait a minute, Dragomine. I saw the Deeps at the Hinge—saw them with my own eyes."

"Yes, that was a test zone. Unfortunately that design broke down almost at once. The installations at East Florida and Hatteras lasted somewhat longer. Theoretically the possibilities were promising, but in actual practice the obstacles were overwhelming, and the project cost was prohibitive. So it was decided at the highest level to postpone further efforts, although research was to continue—as I believe it did over several decades, but no serious project proposal ever emerged from it."

"You're saying that the Deeps don't exist—"

"Exactly."

"—that they never existed—"

"Except for the prototypes, no."

"—that it's all a lie? I can't accept that, Dragomine. I can't believe it. You can explain away what I saw at the Hinge, but not the monitors and sensors I observed every day at Baltimore Canyon—I saw them in other regional control centers, too—and these were hooked into the Deeps system, they were an integral part of it, they registered all the fluctuations, all the changes, everything—"

"The monitors and sensors were set up as a self-enclosed system, Fowke. They evaluate themselves."

"You mean—to fool people like me? To make us think there's something behind them even though there isn't?"

"You might put it that way."

"But—we studied the Deeps in school! There've been hundreds of analyses and reports and seminars—"

"All based on theoretical designs, Fowke. Not the actuality."

My thoughts were in a whirl. I was dazed. He couldn't be lying. Why would he? "Tell me," I said. "Does Dr. Matthews saw about this—this fraud?"

"The Northeast man? No, he wouldn't know. Not at his level. This was restricted to the top people."

"Why are you telling me now?"

"I'm under duress—"

"I'm not threatening you—"

"—and besides, what difference does it make now? All this is past history, of little importance today. People have forgotten about it; they don't really care if there are Deeps or not."

"But the Wall is starting to collapse!"

"It wasn't built to last, Fowke. The official life span has been estimated variously at from one to three thousand years, although the government knew it would be more like two or three hundred—but all that was taken into account, I can assure you. As you know, the population of the affected zones has largely moved West, and the rest will be evacuated when the need arises."

I sat silently staring at him, rage and anguish in my heart. The Wall was dying, it was doomed. It was built on lies. It never had a chance. I gave a choked sob and clenched my fists, which made Dragomine edge back apprehensively.

"What's happening there now?" I asked. "What's happening to the Wall?"

He wiped his forehead with the back of one hand. "I can get the latest reports for you, if you like. I don't keep the details in my head. If you'd let me ask my secretary to put the summaries on the screen—"

"No—and don't move, Dragomine," I said, for he had made a motion as if to go to the door. I couldn't trust him. He'd call security, not his secretary. I had to get out of there, but I didn't know how.

"Do you have a hover here, Dragomine?"

"A hover? Not my own personal hover, no, but there are always several on call in the meadow beyond the Rose Garden." He understood what I wanted. "All you need is my pass card. Here— take it. Just show it to the felid out there. No other identification is necessary."

"I'll need your clothes."

"I'm afraid they won't fit you."

"They'll have to do. Come on—start taking them off."

He removed his jacket and began unbuttoning his shirt, casting uneasy glances at me. I knew he was wondering what was going through my mind: what would I do with *him*? I couldn't take him with me, and if I left him, he'd sound the alarm.

"I can promise you on my honor, Fowke, that I won't stir from this spot for whatever time you say—an hour, two hours—"

"Get those trousers off!"

Stripped to his shorts, Dragomine seemed deflated, humiliated. "What are you going to do to me, Fowke?"

The bathroom door had no outside lock. There was no way I could keep him in and nothing to tie him up with, no rope or cord. I thought of stunning him with the statuette and building a barricade against the bathroom door with the desk and other office furnishings—but then my eye fell on the sections of ursid casing that lay on the floor. That might do it.

"Get into that shell," I told him as I put his shirt on and hastily buttoned it. He gaped at me. "The shell," I said. "Get into it."

"But—I can't."

"Do as I say!"

He picked up the lower section and tried to work one leg into an extensor tube. "It's too tight," he protested. "I can't manage it."

I seized the end of the tube and mercilessly jammed it forward, which made him moan with pain. "Now the rest of it!"

"I can't move, Fowke!"

"That's the idea. Now—the rest of it. Hurry!"

I forced the thoracic casing down over him, wedging him into it, and then fitted the upper extensors on his arms. The parietal casing was easier to fit. Once he was enclosed from head to foot, he lost his sense of balance, tottered a step forward, then fell back full-length with a clatter. "Get me out," his voice came feebly out of the ursid casing. "Please! Get me out of this thing!"

I didn't bother responding. I forced my feet into Dragomine's shoes and left the bathroom, closing the door behind me.

I was lucky. There were no staff people in the outer area, only some office felids, who represented no threat of detection—an

army of Fowkes in ill-fitting suits with ankles and wrists protruding from short trousers and sleeves could have marched past
them unnoticed.

I went into the corridor. I didn't know how to reach the hover
pads. I couldn't hesitate, though. People were passing by, and
some of them glanced at me with curiosity. I went in the direction
I hoped would lead to the rear of the White House—I wasn't
certain of my bearings, I had taken so many turns before—wondering how long it would take Dragomine to crawl out of the
bathroom to raise the alarm.

That corridor angled into another and then a third. At the end
I could see an exit—a door that seemed to lead to the outside,
but there was a human security guard posted beside it. I had no
choice but to continue. As I neared him, I pulled out Dragomine's
pass card. Evidently that was the right thing to do. He made no
move to stop me, and I went past him, opened the door, and
emerged into the White House gardens, blooming brilliantly in
the morning sunlight.

Beyond the flower beds was a large pool, at the edge of which
several persons sat breakfasting at a long table. Farther on was a
meadow where five hovers sat like giant butterflies, the sun golden
on their folded wings.

I walked quickly that way, resisting the temptation to glance
back over my shoulder.

Soon I was near enough to the pool and the breakfast party
to recognize some of the persons there. They included President
Leavit—there could be no mistaking that famous monocle—and
Defense Secretary Guru Armstrong with his bald dome and mut-
tonchop whiskers. Several Secret Service agents were standing
around with their arms crossed, large and powerful figures in dark
suits and sun glasses. Some were looking my way, but they made
no move to intercept me.

I was tense with anxiety, trying to keep a pleasant and busi-
nesslike expression on my face. Time seemed arrested; each step
required an eternity. The air was sweet and fresh, but I was
bothered by the light-dark pattern of sunlight among the shadows
of the trees. Gnats danced before my eyes. I hadn't realized it

before, but I had cut my hand on the ursid shell when I'd forced Dragomine into it; blood was running down my fingers. The Secret Service agents stood with their arms folded watching through their dark glasses, their hats pulled low; the President polished his monocle on his napkin, his head cocked my way. I was dripping blood on the path—in my imagination it seemed a bright red trail that would seize their attention—and, in addition, the jacket was splitting down the back.

The path took me within twenty meters of the Presidential breakfasters. As I went by, I ventured a half-hearted wave and a smile in their direction. The President gave me a puzzled glance but graciously smiled in return. Secretary Armstrong didn't bother looking at me. I kept going at a brisk pace toward the meadow. I could hear their voices behind me. They probably were wondering who I was. They might ask a couple of agents to find out.

No one called out, though. No one came after me.

I reached the meadow and went to the nearest hover, holding up Dragomine's card. The felid-in-charge registered it and opened the door of the hover for me. I climbed in beside the fixed pilot and voxed my destination as Chicago to mislead the FAA flight-plan center.

The pilot started the MOG-blower, and then we rose smoothly straight up. The White House gardens fell away beneath us— meadow, trees, flower beds, the people at the pool, and the pool itself with its pale blue tiles.

It was when we reached the thousand-meter altitude that the recall order came.

The control panel burst into a display of flashing red and orange lights, and a shrill whine came out of the pilot's headphones.

The hover stopped abruptly, then started down.

In the distance I saw four black police hovers whirling up our way, looking as small as horseflies, their sirens screeching.

I made a grab for the stick, but the felid's single grip was locked on it. I couldn't wrest it loose. I jammed my foot underneath the bottom swivel. That at least slowed our descent.

There was a passenger emergency kit in the side pocket. I

snatched out the first thing I found—a signal flare—and ripped off the cap. It burst into wild hot light. I'd intended using its heat to loosen the felid's grip, but I succeeded only in blinding myself and filling the hover cab with sulphurous fumes. I swung open my door and flung the flaming flare out and away.

I wiped the stinging tears from my eyes. The door was still open, flapping in the wind, and the fumes were clearing. I fumbled in the kit for something else. My fingers closed on a wrench. I could see well enough now to begin working at the felid's grip, trying to unbolt it at the nearest joint, the felid equivalent of a human wrist.

The police hovers came swarming around us as I sweated and struggled over the felid's grip-joint. One hover sat above us, the others were at our sides—a box formation. I could see the red-masked and goggled parietals of the pilots glaring across at me. They maintained our rate of descent, escorting us back to the ground.

We actually touched down before I succeeded in detaching the grip.

The loose extensor flopped down. I seized the stick—or rather, the felid's grip, still firmly clamped there—and gave it a powerful shove, sending us rocketing up again. The control panel burst into a rainbow display, and the pilot's headphones shrilled again.

I had to get the felid out of the way. I couldn't maneuver the hover, sprawled across him as I was. I set the stick-lock for a fast climb while I worked at the felid's pinnings with the wrench— the whole seat would have to be removed, since he and it were welded together—every once in a while peering down at the black police hovers rising in angry pursuit.

I freed two bolts, liberating the part of the seat nearest me. I lifted it, swinging the seat and felid up and over as on a hinge, smashing them against the door on the pilot's side—an error in judgment, as this not only buckled the door and shattered the window, it also unbalanced the hover, and we went sawing off at a downward slant, cutting dangerously close to the nearest police hover.

Now I could get behind the controls, and I did so just in time, for the hover was careering away at a tilt, with the felid and part of the seat protruding from the pilot's window, and the air blasting turbulently in all around us.

My only advantage was the fact that I was human, not that my brain would work faster than the instant reaction time of the TR pilots, but that I could do stunts they wouldn't expect. They weren't programmed for recklessness.

I rode my hover, bucking and twisting down to the Mall, veered north toward the New Potomac, the police hot in my wake, and took them dodging among the cherry trees, blowing up showers of pink petals. I had to make my craft jump and back, dart up, down, sideways, to keep them from locking in on me. I made a fast run at the Washington Monument, spinning around the structure in a corkscrew pattern to the top, pausing outside the observation gallery, where I glimpsed placid tourist faces regarding me with interest, as if this were a spectacle arranged for their entertainment. I took the opportunity to scrape off my felid encumbrance against the stone, the way a whale might dislodge a barnacle by rubbing itself on a rock in the sea. The felid, or most of it, went toppling into the gallery among the tourists, while I sent my hover crawling down the side of the Monument like a giant roach, circling as I went to keep out of police range.

I couldn't pause, couldn't plan, couldn't think ahead. I had kicked off Dragomine's tight shoes to free my feet for the horizontal pedal. The jacket had split completely now and flapped loose on my back in the gusts that burst through the open cab. At one point the banging right-hand door finally broke its pins and went sailing off toward the Capitol.

I kept as close to ground level as I could, so they couldn't fire their pellets without endangering pedestrians. I had the impression that the whole city was watching. Traffic had come to a standstill. Office workers craned their heads out of the windows. Even the ursid traffic cops gaped up as I went flashing by, drawing my train of pursuers behind me. But the TR pilots seemed to be learning my tricks. They sent attackers after me in pairs, shooting out their hooks at the same time. It was sheer luck that I managed to dodge them. Now and then one would take a pellet potshot at me. I knew I couldn't last much longer. There were hovers cutting ahead of me now. In a minute or two they would force me down.

Then I saw the Smithsonian Museum directly ahead of me.

I had visited the place several times during my time-killing afternoons in Denver, and I had a pretty good picture of it in my mind—I mean of the historical display of ancient aircraft in the huge exhibition hall—and, as by this time I was desperate as well as reckless, I didn't hesitate. I headed straight for the giant glasstic window and smashed right through.

The air history display is like the Washington original: there must be twenty-five airplanes of all sizes and periods hanging on wires from the ceiling at different levels, so that tourists can gaze up to see them poised, as it were, in suspended flight. These include Lindbergh's "Spirit of St. Louis," the Doolittle bomber, the first space shuttle, the first airdart, and the prototype Ford–Sikorsky T-model hover. It is a unique and irreplaceable collection, which draws large crowds.

I went whirling in there in a shower of pulverized glasstic, with the police hovers right on my tail, and began a dizzy circuit of the place, zigzagging among the suspended antiquities, avoiding them by millimeters. The tourists below ran for the exits—and just in time, too, for the TR pilots, unprogrammed for Smithsonian hazards, paid no attention to the ceiling wires, which were hard to see anyway. I knew the wires were there; they didn't. I suppose they assumed that these apparently airborne machines were simply other kinds of hovers. Where I dodged, they went straight, taking what appeared to be shortcuts. It was a fearful slaughter. Hover after hover sliced into the wires and got snared in them, their MOGs making horrible grinding sounds. They went cartwheeling to the floor, hauling down with them the priceless aerial treasures to smash to bits. Clouds of dust plumed up.

I kept swooping, drawing the surviving hovers to destruction one by one. The floor was littered with smoking rubble. I glimpsed three tiny figures below moving about—murid janitors with whisk-grips and dustpan attachments. Normally they didn't have to deal with anything bigger than a fleck of lint, but here they were confronting mountains by comparison, which they attacked in a hopeless frenzy.

How many TR machines were left? Four . . . five? The Doolittle B-29 plummetted to the floor, taking two hapless hovers with it. Another attacker got hung up in the wires of the Goodyear football blimp and remained caught above it like a buzzing black beetle trapped in the web of a fat white spider. One pursuing hover ran afoul of the World War II Spitfire's suspension, jolting the pilot forward against his stick. He shot straight up and smashed through the glasstic dome. I could see his wreckage as a blurred mothlike shadow as it tumbled down the slope of the dome outside.

One hover left. The last. I dodged beneath Lindbergh's venerable plane. The TR, chasing me, smacked blindly into it from the rear, ripping its wires free as he plunged deep into the fuselage, and bore the entire relic away with him in his impetus. As I wheeled around and made my exit through the gap in the shattered window I had created when I entered, I was followed into the open air outside by this apparition: "The Spirit of St. Louis" in its final flight—pilotless, its propellers idly turning in the wind as it soared in my wake, a ghost from centuries past. It pursued me above the streets—only by chance, for the TR pilot, buried with his hover inside, must have had his sensors blocked.

At the FBI building, I swerved to one side. The "Spirit" made its final spurt, flying head-on into the stocky statue of the agency's founder, cleaving it neatly at the crotch, leaving the bronze legs firmly planted on the base. The rest fetched up with the wreckage of the "Spirit" and the hover it contained in a smoking mass at the base of the FBI flagpole.

I raced off at top speed, anxious to leave the Federal area before fresh police hovers arrived. I skimmed the tops of buildings and cut along the canyons of the streets until I reached the lower bend of the New Potomac, beyond the Denver Generation Center. I used the river as a guide, whirring low over the water and cutting beneath the bridges, staying as much as possible in the leafy shadows of the bank-side trees in order to minimize detection from the air. I glimpsed dots overhead. More hovers, searching for me.

On the outskirts of the metropolitan area, I found what I'd been looking for—the air cargo port, where dozens of skytrucks arrive and leave each hour, bearing freight to and from every major center in the nation. It is a complex of landing fields and warehouses, centered around the international shootsite; glassways and monotracks run off in every direction. The whole place rumbles with activity.

I had little time. Those dots were getting larger. They had homed in on me. I touched down at the edge of the nearest strip, pausing in the high grass. Some two hundred meters dead ahead was a skytruck getting ready to lift. Its MOGs were warming up, and its conical nose was rising. This was my best chance. I shot forward at my top speed, running just above the tarmac, approaching the ST from the rear. It began to lift. In a few seconds it would be beyond me, gathering speed far faster than I could go—and the racing police hovers would be on top of me.

It was a close thing. I came within hook range, half-blinded by the billowing air exhaust of the ST's MOGs. Lifting my hover as the giant truck rose, maneuvering for the right position, and aware of the screaming descent of the first black hovers, I made my launch, aiming for the ST's notched tailfin, hooked and held, and braced myself for the full takeoff blast.

The battered little hover and I were jerked aloft, leaping upward with the ST's powerful thrust, like a flea on an eagle's tail. The field vanished, the hovers scattered below us. We barreled up toward the sun.

I wasn't prepared for the force of the climb. It plastered me flat against the back of the cab. I couldn't even blink my eyelids. This effect diminished when the trajectory began to level off, but by then we were so high that the oxygen was thinning, and the cold was paralyzing. I was stunned, helpless, blacking out. If the hook-cable hadn't broken under the strain, I would have arrived as a corpse at whatever destination the ST was bound for.

The hover went fluttering down like a leaf, while I banged around inside the cab, semi-conscious, barely managing to keep from being tossed out the open side. Everything loose flew out—Dragomine's shoes, the wrench, the emergency kit, the pilot seat-bolts. Dizzy and sick, I fumbled at the controls with sleepwalker's hands and got the balloons out just in time. We settled down in a field of cabbages. I staggered out of the cab, fell down and slept for a while, then woke ravenously hungry and ate a cabbage, roots and all. I had no idea where I was. I didn't know what direction the ST had been going. I would have stayed in the field a little longer to rest if a farm-murid hadn't come into view—one of those little globular ones with eight extensors (bug-pickers, they are called). When it saw me, it began to squeal, whirled around, and went hopping off, no doubt to report my presence to its felid.

I got the hover going and went off at a low altitude, heading east.

An hour later, I came to a huge river I thought might be the Mississippi. I followed it south until I recognized a type of channel guide we'd used below Memphis when I was running the Interchange System. The ST must have been bound for New Orleans to have carried me this far southeast.

I crossed the river and kept going east until dark, taking care to avoid cities and towns, and flying beneath the ridgeline of hills to minimize the danger of being picked up on the RTR screens.

At sundown I parked in the branches of an enormous oak in what I think are the Great Smokies—range after range of blue-gray forested mountains.

That's where I am now. I have just finished writing my account of what has happened since yesterday afternoon, when I put on the ursid shell back in Denver.

It is a clear night, and I could run the hover on moonlight, but it is battered and bent, and the MOG has been wheezing. It needs a rest. So do I.

At dawn I will head east again. I should reach the Shelf by noon.

MAY 30

The day is bright and still, no wind, no clouds. The sunlight fills the sky. I am hovering east across Georgia. The fragrance of the earth rises in the heat: the orchards, the farmlands, the pine forests. I have just crossed the Atlanta–Jacksonville glassway.

In the distance I can see two faint lines running parallel against the horizon—Rampart and Wall! Still standing!

Soon I will reach the old coastline, somewhere south of Savannah.

I have touched down in a grove of palmettos in what was once one of the Sea Islands.

It is an island again.

When I first saw the East Georgia Shelf, it looked just as I had hoped it would—a vast flatland stretching east toward the hazy smudgeline that marked the Rampart ridge. The light of the sun reflected off this great expanse, and I couldn't make out any of the details: the roads, the farm buildings, the occasional town.

Only when I got closer did I realize that there were no details. No roads, no towns—no land. It was water that had caught the sun. All water.

The Shelf has disappeared.

JUNE 1

I share this island with pelicans and gulls, crabs, turtles, and sandpipers. We fish together, side by side, walk the beach, swim, wade in the shallows.

At first I saw no signs of what had been here before the waters returned. The shock of it must have blinded me. But now I have begun to notice ... the top of a silo some two hundred meters east that just breaks the surface (I'd thought it was a rock) ... the submerged fence posts that run between this island and the next, white as whalebone in the water ... the carcass of a farm felid I found on the south shore, half-buried in the sand, crusted with barnacles.

There is a tremendous quiet here, broken only by the cries of the birds. The sea is placid; it merely laps the shore. From here, at ground level, I cannot see the Rampart and the Wall, and sometimes I wonder if I imagined seeing them when I approached by air, but the calmness of the waters is evidence that they exist. This is not an ocean shore; it is a giant lagoon. How far does it extend? What happened in Florida? And what has happened north of here?

These questions trouble me, and I wonder about them, but they don't obsess me, otherwise I would be beating up the coast in the hover, frantically searching. It's not that I don't care or that I'm afraid to find out the truth. Perhaps it's the shock, the feeling of awe I have here on this island that was a hill overlooking a valley of farms and orchards where the sea has come back, not as a raging vengeful god, but in peace, simply restoring what had been before.

JUNE 2

I am in Savannah. As far as I can tell, I am the only human here.

This morning I got the hover going again and rose up above my little island until I could see the double line of Rampart and Wall on the horizon—I hadn't imagined them, after all—and flew toward them across the great Shelf lagoon.

Both structures appear undamaged, except there is heavy erosion evident on the Rampart's eastern flank. I noticed the cause at once. In contrast to the placidity of the lagoon, the waters that now cover the flatland area between Rampart and Wall are sealike, surging and boiling, as if driven by powerful currents. These appear to come from the south, which would give substance to

Dr. Grandgent's report of a break in Florida. The lagoon water level is ten or fifteen meters below that covering the flatlands, indicating that the Rampart has held to a considerable extent, at least in this zone.

I landed atop the Wall—no easy trick in a lopsided hover with the treacherous ocean breezes tugging and shoving. I wanted to feel it beneath my feel again, to touch it, to draw from it that strength it has always given me...even more so now that it is wounded, perhaps mortally, and yet still stands.

Flying north above the lagoon, I could look down and see beneath the surface of the water the wavering outlines of roads, houses, barns and sheds, sunken forests...a whole landscape hidden down there. Here and there on higher ground a roof would show above the surface. Once I saw part of a small town sticking up— a few houses and a store, half-submerged, roads running just beneath the surface, and floating debris shifting in the gentle wash of the lagoon.

Nowhere did I see a living soul.

In mid-afternoon I reached Savannah, an abandoned city. Water up to the second stories—a dead waste of sluggish brown water, unlike the fresh clear water of the lagoon. It hadn't been there long. The trees were dying but still alive. Savannah was silent, rotting in the heat. A sickly miasma hung over everything. I could see water snakes knotting and wriggling at the edges of the houses; there were fish down there, too, but not the kinds of fish anybody would want to eat.

I hovered back and forth above the rooftops. Where were the people? Had they all gotten away? Alligators cruised the streets. Owls nested in the attics. On the roof of a bank I saw six murids standing motionless, waiting for instructions that would never come. The hum of my hover drew their attention. Their heads rotated in unison as I circled above them and remained fixed in my direction as I flew away.

JUNE 3

I am worried about Julia. I wonder what has happened to her.
If the Northeast has been hit in a break—it could be far worse
in Atlantis North than what I've seen down here—her station
could have been caught in it and wiped out in a sudden tremendous punch of the sea. Maybe there was enough warning so
people could get out; maybe she was somewhere else, farther
inland.

Charleston, too, is a ghost city, half-drowned, empty of life.
   I settled down on the roof of an office building, found a trap
door by the water tank, and descended the stairs inside, inspecting
the top floors which were above water, calling out as I went, in
case there were any stranded humans there; no one answered.
The building housed various commercial enterprises, to judge by
what I found. I salvaged a Librex from one office, several cans
of peanut snacks from another. There were no signs that the
occupants had left in haste. Everything seemed orderly, chairs
neatly pushed in, desks clear, terminals closed. I found a telemin
still in place in a corner office and used it to call the Atlantis
North DIPS station—got the buzz that means out of service. I
then called DIPS Central, trying to locate her, but they wouldn't
give out any information. As a message I left the name I'd used
when I had VXed her from Denver: T. O. Wall.

The farther north I go, the more turbulent the waters become.
Heavy currents clash in the Wilmington Valley, whipping the
surface and boiling up dark stains of mud. Debris—branches,
building timbers, highway markers, fence posts—is scattered
everywhere, swirling in the eddies.
   Wilmington itself has a battered look: buildings caved in, the
watery streets clogged with wreckage, street lamps bent, trees
uprooted and floating about.
   I made a circuit inland to have a look at the countryside beyond

the flood line. There were no vehicles moving on the roads, and the towns seemed empty, except for one, about fifty kilometers north, where I saw a dozen people moving about. When they saw my hover approaching, they scattered, running into the nearest houses to hide. I saw a woman snatch up a small child and carry it inside. Only excluded would behave like that—or have children with them. Most other people must have had time to escape inland when the ocean started coming in, and excluded colonies like the one in Baltimore may have gotten away, too.

But what about those that were fenced in like the one northeast of Boston? Did anyone bother to let them go?

I wonder what happened up there.

JUNE 4

At Hatteras I saw the effects of what must have been a full-scale rip.

The Wall is shattered—a gap two kilometers wide—and the Rampart behind it is smashed. From above it looks as if a giant fist had slammed through them both with one tremendous punch. The force of the rip scoured deep inland, digging a huge trench.

The ocean surges through this great opening, chewing at the sides, plunging back and forth with its tides and currents. As I circled overhead in the hover, I saw great chunks of Rampart slide into the sea, carrying roadways and houses and whole groves of trees. The Wall, more resistant, is eroding at a lesser rate. Now and then a small section of hydrofex splits and crumbles.

It is a terrible sight—and yet what amazes me is how the destruction remains limited to this one area. On either side of the gap, the Wall stretches away along the horizon in a solid and unbroken line. It must be gravely weakened, though. Other sections could go at any time. Everything I know from my training and experience tells me that the Wall cannot last long, once breached.

*   *   *

Only now, hours after I first saw the Hatteras rip, have I realized what has been destroyed.

Hatteras weather is notoriously violent and unpredictable. McKay was strongly criticized for choosing this area for his administrative headquarters (it was first located on the mainland, near Washington, N.C., but was moved east as progressive stages of the project were completed, to Pamlico, then to the old Cape itself, and finally—long after Mckay's death, of course—to the East Scarp). McKay was unmoved by these protests. He chose Hatteras deliberately, to show his defiance of the elements.

I visited the East Scarp several years ago. It had become a national historical landmark, with a museum in which early equipment was on display, together with blueprints and drawings and a scale model of the entire project, where visitors could observe a miniature Atlantic pounding against a miniature Wall.

Nearby were modern administrative buildings and a large tourist center with cottages and hotels, also a retirement complex for aging engineers who had worked on the System in its final stages. A special glassway spur had been built to serve the Scarp, a small city with a population of twelve thousand people.

On top of the Scarp, above the hotels and cottages, above the museum and the retirement complex, McKay's tomb was built in accordance with the designs he made before his death—a sixty-meter peak of granite faced with black marble, surmounted by a giant statue of himself (the tiny replica of which I used to threaten Dragomine in the White House), arms flung wide and head challengingly thrust forward. His remains were sealed in the base of this huge figure.

All this has been swept away.

The Scarp has vanished.

JUNE 8

I have set the hover down on top of the Neptune city hall, three meters above the flood wash.

*　　*　　*

On my way north I saw three bodies—human bodies—swollen corpses floating on the surface of the water that covers the Chesapeake Valley.

The pattern of flooding along the Shelf defies logic. In places, the breaks appear total—vast sections of Wall and Rampart smashed and crumbling or vanished outright—and here the ocean has driven a dozen or more kilometers inland beyond the old coastline. Elsewhere—East Georgia and the Chesapeake Valley— the Wall stands unbroken, and the Atlantic has seeped in by slow degrees, forming giant lagoons which vary both in depth and extent. In still other places, the inner rim of the Shelf valley remains dry, at least for now. But everything is changing. Tides and storms beat in. Powerful currents run in contrary directions and in unexpected sequences; the surface of a lagoon that appears calm will suddenly be broken by a wild wave that rises out of nowhere, rushing fiercely north or west or east toward the sea.

There are no norms, no guides. It is chaos—a frightening and unpredictable maelstrom. Splendid in its way, a terrifying splendor.

I have the sensation that underneath these ferocious shifts and surges there is something permanent and unchanging. The coast will not go back to what it was before.

The Wall and Rampart here in Baltimore Canyon are virtually intact. The flatlands are flooded, of course, but inland from the Rampart—Neptune and its environs—the water is surprisingly low, perhaps six meters in depth.

I put down my water skids and skated the hover across the sunken town, looking down at my old office and then locating Gorton Avenue and following it to my house. I anchored there and stripped and dived down for a closer look. The windows were broken. Fish swam in and out. The living room furniture was turning in the currents, the lighter pieces bobbing against the ceiling. Hilda's neural pictures still hung on the walls, and the Vidipix had been left on. It was showing the felid Rockettes in synchronized dance routines.

JUNE 18

I have established a camp in one of the abandoned houses on the Rampart. Other tenants, with greater seniority, are owls and chipmunks and a family of raccoons. We try to ignore one another. In a second-story room with a view of the Wall I have laid a bed of pine boughs and sheaves of wild grass and installed my Librex on a little packing crate I found washed up along the flatlands shore. From a warehouse in South Poseidon, where I hovered several days ago, I salvaged boxes of canned fruit and vegetables and various other things: knives, tools, rope, and a magnifying glass for igniting fires.

I have rigged up some fishing tackle—electric cable with a bent fork as a hook—and I fish the flatlands from the idling hover. I dig clams along the shore. There are blue crabs, too.

A more ambitious project is building a boat. It will be a sort of raft: logs lashed together with rope and cable, with a platform on top. I am shaping a pair of wooden oars.

And I have made a weapon—a sling—just in case.

JUNE 19

Every day I hover across the reach of choppy salt water that covers the flatlands and take a look at the Wall. I am tempted to touch down on top but haven't dared yet. The winds are treacherous up there. A sudden gust could topple my hover. It is showing signs of wear as it is and could use a maintenance check—which it won't get. I'm not sure how long it will last.

PART
SEVEN

JUNE 22

Something is happening in the Wall, although there are no visible signs.

It looks the same as ever, and the water levels appear to be unchanged since my arrival here. Still . . . something is happening in there.

I have patroled the whole zone all the way from Chesapeake to the Hudson Towers, inspecting both the ocean and the inland sides, hovering as close and as low as conditions permit, and idling in place whenever I've seen anything that might be the beginning of a fissure, and it all seems solid and sound, and yet, sometimes when I've cut the MOG to a whisper, I've become aware of strange sounds, a series of low rumblings, and then again, in other places, a steady noise almost like a prolonged groan.

JUNE 24

Today I took my boat out for the first time. I dragged it down to the flatland shore, hauled it out into the water, scrambled up

217

on top, fitted my oars into the forked-branch oarlocks, and began rowing across. I had no idea of going all the way to the Wall, but I struck a favorable current that pushed me along, and after an hour I realized I was closer to the Wall than to the Rampart, so I rowed the rest of the way.

I found the place where the old rungs went up, tied the boat to the lowest one, and started to climb. I got a third of the way up when I heard the sound of a hover in the sky. That meant police to me. It didn't sound close, and I couldn't pick it out of the sky when I craned around for a look, but I decided not to wait for it. I jumped into the water, a forty-meter plunge that knocked the breath out of me, and came up gasping and blowing to hide behind my boat, peering up for the hover.

I couldn't see it, and I couldn't hear it any longer. It had come from the west—from the direction of the Rampart. I climbed into the boat to dry off in the sun. Had it gone away? I couldn't be sure, and I couldn't risk starting back across the flatlands, ten kilometers of choppy water with the current against me this time. It would take me hours of blistering labor with the oars, and if the hover returned and caught me out there, I'd have little chance. I had to wait.

I used my time pulling vines and seaweed off the Wall to drape over my boat, trying to make it look like a piece of wreckage. The sun beat down hard. I had come out without food and water. There were mussels clinging to the Wall at the waterline. I pried some off and beat them open against the Wall, drank them down. That took the edge off my thirst.

Now the hover reappeared. It sprang up from the Rampart ridge, no bigger than a speck at that distance, circled a few times and then went north, vanishing from sight.

It was dusk when I reached the Rampart shore. I hauled my boat up into the bushes, tied it to a tree, and walked up the slope to my house.

I knew something was wrong. Even in the dimming light I could see that the only unbroken window in the place—the one in the room I'd chosen for myself—had been knocked out. And then I saw that my bedding—the boughs and grass sheaves—had been flung out and scattered over the ground. I hurried up the stairs. My room was a wreck. The Librex lay upside-down in a corner, its panel wrenched off. My stores of food were strewn everywhere.

I thought of my hover. I ran back downstairs and outside, fighting through the dark brush to the little clearing where it was parked.

It was broken, too. Its wings bent, its windshield scarred as if beaten by rocks, and the MOG had been split in a dozen places. I saw at a glance that the hover was damaged beyond repair.

JUNE 25

What few things I have left I have moved to a thicket of wild privet a kilometer north, near the ridge line, where I am building a lean-to shelter that can't be seen from the air. Nearby is a natural lookout tower: a tall maple, thickly leaved.

The pilot of that hover must have been human. If a TR had been programmed to do what was done to my possessions, the destruction would have been total. This was an act of viciousness and malice, something almost personal in its spitefulness. And— if the object had been to capture me—it was stupid, too. Having located my camp, he should have called in a few others to drop down on me at dawn and take me by surprise. But now I am warned.

He will be back. I am watching for him. Will he come alone or with others? I wonder, *are* there any others?

I am practicing with my sling. I am accurate within thirty paces. Gulls serve as moving targets. I knocked down three of five today.

JUNE 27

The hover came back today. It cut in low from the western side of the Rampart, skimming the trees, and I just had time to duck into one of the tunnels I have cut in the privet to avoid being spotted, for it passed directly overhead. I crawled through to the other side and climbed the maple. In another minute the hover reappeared, making a return swing over the area, systematically searching for me. It didn't look like a police hover, but it was an official one, certainly, for it had a government serial number on the side. I caught a glimpse of the pilot as he peered down in his cap and goggles.

I waited for other hovers to appear. God knows what they will do. They could airdrop an ursid if they have one.

It is the end of the day. Sundown. The hover spent an hour droning around over this part of the Rampart but didn't land. Nor did any other hovers show up.

If he returns tomorrow—alone—I'll be ready for him.

JUNE 28

Just past nine o'clock this morning I heard the hum of the hover from the west and scrambled up to my lookout post in the tree. Same hover, same pattern of low flight, with hanging pauses now and then, same pilot's goggled head craning out to look down. There were no other hovers in sight.

I shinnied to the ground and ran through the woods to my old house. I took up a position in the clearing where my wrecked hover sat. I put myself in plain view deliberately, to lure the pilot into sling range.

When he passed over, I waved up at him. He did a quick circle and returned, tilting to one side to get a good downward look at me. I was still waving my arms in a beckoning movement—and he waved back. It struck me at the time as an ironic gesture.

He started down, slowly settling toward the center of the clearing.

When the hover was about ten meters above me, I loaded my sling and let fly a jagged rock the size of a cantaloupe. It sheared off one of the rear stabilizers, and the hover dipped its nose and slanted sideways.

I loaded and slung, loaded and slung, as rapidly as I could.

One rock smacked a wing. The next struck amidships, jolting the hover off balance.

I could see the pilot struggling with the controls and apparently shouting down at me—the hum of the MOG drowned out his voice—and once shaking a gloved fist angrily.

I had reloaded, but no further shots were required. The crippled craft was out of control. The balloons went out—too late. The hover slipped slowly into a pair of oaks, its wings chewing branches to splinters, and came thrashing down from limb to limb to end nose-first on the ground next to the remains of my own ruined machine.

I ran over to haul out the pilot and overpower him, when I was stopped short by a furious voice:

"Fowke—you idiot! Look what you've done! Fool!"

I knew the voice. It wasn't a man's.

The pilot, unhurt, leaped out of the wreckage and tore off her cap and goggles.

It was Julia, boiling with rage.

I stood in astonishment, too amazed to move. And then I was seized by a kind of wild joy which (even as she berated me) brought tears to my eyes and spread what I suspect was an idiotic grin across my face, which probably infuriated her all the more. All I could think of was that she was here—Julia was here with me—and I wasn't alone any more.

It is the middle of the night. Julia is sleeping wrapped in a parachute salvaged from the wreck. I am too worried to sleep. To make matters worse, a heavy shower at sundown drenched us both and extinguished the cooking fire. The fish was half-raw, and she refused to eat her portion. I must admit that her ill temper is not unjustified, even though my mistake was one anybody in my position might have made.

The question remains—who was the pilot of that first hover, the one who destroyed my camp? And . . . will he come back?

JUNE 29

Julia's anger has subsided into a heavy sullenness, not improved by the fact that she caught cold last night. I went down to the shore at daybreak to dig clams and prepared a stew which didn't appeal to her for some reason. I ate it all myself.

Her hover sprawls at the base of the oaks, a monument to my rashness. She told me she'd been searching for me ever since she got my first message and that the hover was to carry us to Mexico. Now what?

I have sworn I will repair it, using spare parts from my own machine. But I don't think I can do it. I know next to nothing about the workings of these craft. To make a show of effort, I have poked through the wreckage, examining the bent and broken parts with a studious expression but with despair in my heart.

Julia has recounted what she knows about damage along the Northeast Shelf.

A rip broke the Wall at the Portsmouth Extension a month ago, flooding part of Boston and most other cities along the old coast as far south as Plymouth and wiping out Cape Cod, Martha's Vineyard and Nantucket.

She heard, but can't confirm, that the Wall north of Portsmouth has held.

The rip touched off a panic evacuation. Her unit was lifted out of its Truro base just in time. It was relocated in Brockton, but only as a formality, for all personnel fled west, leaving stores and equipment. Other federal and state agencies and commercial establishments did the same.

In the entire Northeast, organized society has ceased to exist. No government, no population, nothing.

She got her hover from an abandoned air park in Brockton. There were dozens of them for the taking—and there'd be plenty still in other air parks, too, if only we could get to the mainland.

But how? We are separated from the coast by what must be more than one hundred and fifty kilometers of salt water.

Thinking to encourage her, I took her to the shore and showed her my little boat, explaining that I would build another one big enough for both of us.

"You must be out of your mind," was all she had to say.

She may be right.

I have said nothing to her about the sounds I heard from the interior of the Wall.

JULY 4

Yesterday by a lucky stroke I managed to repair the Librex— "repair" in a manner of speaking, for it operates in fits and starts, and half the time it will retrieve things you haven't asked for, like an old dog with dim vision. I have been trying to get it to find the Basic Hover Repair Manual, and instead it has brought me screens from a Finnish cookbook and some chess problems.

JULY 5

As Julia's anger has passed, so has her sullenness. She is quiet. Maybe grim would be a better description. She takes up her daily tasks with determination, as if by absorbing herself in them she can avoid thinking about other things.

We are both busy all day. I go off to fish and dig clams. She picks berries and weaves fishing nets from reeds. I work on the new boat, and she collects wood for our cooking fires. We meet for meals and sometimes work on projects requiring joint effort—

stripping shingles off an abandoned house for the lean-to, for example—but we speak only of our immediate practical problems, avoiding all deeper and more puzzling questions.

What weighs on us is the knowledge that each word or act can have a significance—can have consequences—for which neither of us is prepared.

We sleep separately, she in the lean-to, I on a grass bed outside. When it rains, I move inside to the corner opposite hers. We have separate sanitary pits, too, and by tacit agreement, she bathes at the inland shore, while I go down to the flatland side.

Sometimes we catch ourselves looking at each other, troubled and at a loss, trying to understand things we have never had to deal with before.

We are marooned psychologically, too.

JULY 6

The ocean that has trapped us here extends north and south as far as the eye can see. Sometimes the water laps at the shore, sometimes it is whipped by storm and current into slashing breakers. Even on sunny days, the sea on the inland side may be disturbed by sudden swells that originate far to the north or south, where the Rampart is breached, any one of which would be powerful enough to swamp a stronger boat than the one I am putting together. I watch these deadly surges with foreboding.

JULY 7

Our habitat, the Rampart, is an artificial reinforced-earth dam which over the years has been transformed by the natural workings of seed and insect and wandering animals. The original plantings of trees are now lush and high—oak and maple, birch, pine, and fir—and they have been supplemented by migrants of all kinds: spruce, chestnut, elm, poplar, and walnut, shrubs and vines and wildflowers scattered among the weeds and grasses in the open places. There are colonies of bees and empires of ants—and storms of mosquitoes that rise from the shore at dusk on these hot summer days to drive us inside the lean-to until, with the onset of night, they vanish.

We live among songbirds—and the hawks that feed on them. There are owls, woodpeckers, larks and swallows, and, of course, sea birds, chief among them the herring gull. The largest animals are the raccoons. There are field mice, chipmunks and squirrels. I have seen no rabbits and no grouse or wild turkeys.

For us, the most important inhabitants of this place are the fish.

I have located three hives, but I have no idea how to get the honey without being stung. I tried to coax some information out of the Librex, but it perversely offered me screens on curing hams and treating cattle for gas-bloat.

I am used to a rough life, but Julia has never known physical hardship, and it must be changing her as it has changed me. At least it is changing what I see. That jaunty confidence—the manner of the competent and arrogant DIPS agent—that is gone. She seems wary; there is uncertainty in her gaze. Every day she has to do things she is totally unprepared to do. Simple things: make a fire, wash clothes, scale fish. Her inexperience makes her blunder. Sometimes she seems ready to weep with vexation and weariness. She looks different, too. The sun has darkened her face and roughened her skin. Her hair has lost its gloss; it is curled and tangled now. I like it better that way.

Her pride is still there, though. She has courage and learns fast. Already she is a better shot than I am with the sling. The first time she knocked down a lark, she burst into tears. But she reloaded and hit another one, and she insisted on doing the dirty work of plucking and gutting them.

We manage well enough now in summer, but what will happen when the seasons change? We must at all costs get back to the mainland. Work on the boat progresses slowly. It takes me days to fell and trim a tree of the size needed for the raftlike hull.

Ripping boards and salvaging nails from the abandoned houses for use in the superstructure takes many hours.

The boat should be ready soon, though. It is our only hope. I have abandoned the pretense of trying to repair one of the hovers. She realizes the impossibility of this, I think. We no longer mention the subject.

I still think of the other hover—it must be from the police—and watch for it.

We live like savages, working with our hands and the tools our hands have made, but we are not savages in our minds. How can I put it? We are creatures of our times. For many years—generations—the social ideal has been to keep people apart because of the dangers of letting them satisfy their sensory and emotional needs on one another, but here we have none of the technology of gratification: no comforter, no stimulator, no Juvenor, not even the distraction of a sonex, nor the creative stimulus of a neural art connection. We stand face to face, unprotected. The threat of aggressivity hangs over us. When by chance, working together, our hands make contact, we quickly pull back. It is too risky.

And yet we need closeness and comfort, we need to touch. What restrains us is the fear of the unknown. We don't know what to do. We are afraid to take a first step. We are like children in our ignorance, animals in our fear. We avoid each other's eyes.

JULY 8

I decided to go to the Wall today. Julia didn't want to make the trip—can't say I blame her, as it is a brutal pull across all that water—and I wasn't surprised when she said she'd stay here. I don't know how I could have fitted her into the single-seater boat, anyway.

I think she is relieved at the prospect of having a day to herself.

* * *

The sun was halfway up the morning sky when I got started. I had rigged up a small sail—an old window curtain stiffened by reeds, tied to a poplar mast—but it didn't help. It kept swinging around and knocking against my shoulders, so I finally pulled the damned thing down. Besides, there wasn't much of a breeze. It was steamy hot. The July sun baked down, and mist obscured my vision of the Wall, even when I got fairly near. I steered toward the sun, with the sweat flushing out of me and the oars groaning and my arms and shoulders aching from the strain. Gulls circled high overhead, laughing at me. Sometimes one would flutter down to ride the swells just out of oar-reach, looking at me sideways.

It was past noon when I reached the Wall—and then I had to spend a long time searching for the place where the rungs were, since I'd veered off course in the mist. I tied the boat to the lowest rung and started up. It was a hard climb under any circumstances, and I was already worn down from the trip. I had to stop several times to rest, and I seemed to hear the sounds I'd heard before coming from deep within the Wall, as if the Wall were echoing me, straining from the pressure, straining from the weight, its supports eroded by all the storms of all these years. A hollow sort of sound it was, that low moaning having changed into something deeper and duller, like the prolonged note of a gigantic muffled bell, and I had the sensation that I was clinging to an enormous shell of stone that continued to resist the pounding of the Atlantic by sheer will.

I reached the top, drained and spent, just sat there panting and wiping away the sweat. The mist was clearing. I could see the Rampart ridgeline now, could even pick out the crown of that big maple I used as an observation tower.

On the ocean side, the endless water swelled and sank, boiling over the breakwater, hidden now by the tide. I had a moment of giddiness, seeming to feel the Wall tilt beneath me, starting to bear me down—but it was only the heat. I sat resting with my head bowed and my arms crossed on top of my knees.

I don't know how long I stayed like that. The air was heavy and damp. The sun came slamming down; there was no breeze, no shade. I heard the cries of the gulls and the slow slap of the ocean against the Wall. I heard a humming, too, dim at first, then louder, and if I thought about it at all in my drowsiness, I probably thought it came from inside my head, which was buzzing with heat and fatigue.

And then it was there—the hover—not twenty meters away.

It had landed on top of the Wall, and the pilot was climbing out.

He was human, not a TR, and he carried a riot stick in one hand, an ugly black cylinder about a meter in length.

I recognized him at once—those pink plump cheeks, the scraggly sand-colored mustache. It was Dr. Matthews.

He was advancing slowly, squinting at me in a surly, puzzled way. "You're Fowke," he said, but I could tell he wasn't sure, and I didn't wonder, skinny and scarred as I was, with a month's growth of hair and beard. The remains of Dragomine's suit clung to me in rags.

I had risen to my feet. We stood facing each other under that brutal sun, while the ocean lapped on both sides of the Wall far beneath us.

"I'm glad you came, Dr. Matthews," I said. I tried to muster up a friendly and unconcerned manner to put him off guard, but my voice came out a croak. "There's another person with me— over there." I pointed toward the distant Rampart. "We don't have any way of getting to the mainland. Something happened to the hover I had."

He was staring at me suspiciously, tapping the riot stick against the palm of his hand. (If it had been turned on, it would have given him such a jolt he'd have been knocked flat. I saw it happen once to a forgetful security officer in a training film.)

"I'll get you to the mainland, all right," he muttered. "Don't worry about that. And who's that other person you've got? Or is that one of your lies?"

"It isn't an excluded. It's a woman, and she's a citizen, with full rights. I'll tell you where she is, and you can fly her out and then come back for me."

He gave a little laugh. "I can see through your trick, Fowke.

Don't think I can't. You want to send me off on a wild-goose chase looking for this nonexistent person so you'll have a chance to escape again, isn't that it?"

"No, I swear she's there. She happens to be a DIPS agent—"

"I know you're lying. I saw your hideout. There wasn't any sign of another person. You're alone."

"She wasn't there then. She came a few days after that. If you hadn't wrecked my hover, she'd be safe now."

"*You'd* be safe, Fowke. That's what you really mean."

I glanced at his hover. It was that I wanted, if I had to toss him into the ocean to get it. But the odds were against me. That riot stick would fell an ox with a mere touch.

"You'd be on the mainland now, Fowke—in a maximum security detention camp—if the police weren't so inefficient. The moment I spotted your hover, I called them. I waited and waited, but they didn't come." He threw me an aggrieved look, as though expecting me to share his outrage. "I finally had to set down and do the job myself, to make sure you wouldn't escape. And now where are they?" He glanced impatiently around the horizon. "I called them again ten minutes ago, when I saw you up here. That's plenty of time for a fast hover to get here from the South Poseidon station."

"The South Poseidon station is under a good deal of sea water, Dr. Matthews."

"Nonsense! It's sheer laziness and lack of proper command coordination. I can guarantee you I'll file a jot on them that will take the hide off their backs!"

"I don't think the civil services in this area are functioning too well at the moment."

"Not functioning? I won't accept excuses! Why shouldn't they be functioning?"

"Just take a look around you."

He stood fuming and muttering under his breath. "This is just a temporary condition. You see a little water and you jump to conclusions—totally unwarranted conclusions!—because you don't have access to the full systems information flow, as I have, and I can tell you that the real situation is quite different from what you think it is. In a few weeks—a couple of months at most—things will be back to normal, and my position will be totally vindicated by the facts!"

He was nodding to himself and tapping the end of the stick in his hand and glancing around at the ocean with his eyes drawn in a squint, as if refusing to allow its full extent to be registered by his vision. If I'd had my strength, I would have rushed him then. But I was afraid I couldn't move fast enough. I was still dizzy from the sun, which played tricks with my sight. I saw circles of light and little brown specks, and my head was throbbing with the heat.

"... the technology isn't at fault," he was saying. "It's the human element—that's where the trouble lies. If I'd had TR staff work behind me, I'd have easily surmounted this little setback!"

"I reported seepage to you a year ago, but you wouldn't listen."

"Of course I wouldn't. There wasn't any seepage."

"No seepage? What do you think this is—a heavy dew?"

"There was no seepage then!"

"If you hadn't ignored my warnings, something might have been done—!"

"Nothing needed to be done! Everything is automatic and instantaneous! The system have operated perfectly!" Dr. Matthews's face was mottled with heat and anger, and he was breathing hoarsely. I had noticed that he hadn't shaved in days and that his clothing was rumpled and dirty. Perspiration stained his shirt. "The systems don't lie!" he barked at me. "It's men that lie! Men like you! I should have known you'd be a troublemaker, with your genetic defects! It's you who've put that black mark on my record! They blamed me for your ineptness—for your insubordination—your sabotage! They said I should have stopped you sooner! Oh, they didn't say it in so many words, but I know that's what they thought. I was too lenient with you. I temporized. But how was I to know you'd try to go over my head—discredit the whole system—to undercut me and disgrace me...!"

One of the brown specks that plagued my vision was growing

larger. It appeared to be at Wall-top level, far behind Dr. Matthews and his hover.

"...I turned you in too late, Fowke!"

"I figured you were the one."

"Omaha wanted to let you off with administrative discipline and transfer, but I insisted—I threatened to resign if they didn't act—I wouldn't let them give you a mere slap on the wrist! And I made sure they got that accomplice of yours—the brains behind it all—"

"You don't mean Dr. Grandgent?"

"That old fox! He had it in for me ever since my student days! Gave me a C-minus on my M-E finals! Wouldn't recommend me for the Control Board staff! That's why I couldn't get above field level!"

That brown speck had increased in size. It was coming steadily closer. I could see what it was now.

Dr. Matthews began approaching me, extending the riot stick. He snapped it on. Its tip glowed red. "You'll pay for this, Fowke!" he yelled. "It's all your fault!"

I didn't know whether he meant to stun me with the stick or force me over the edge. The inland side was preferable, if I had to make a choice, but I doubted I'd survive a fall from that height.

"Better look behind you, Dr. Matthews."

"None of your tricks!"

I scooped up a handful of Wall detritus—sand, dead lichen flakes and seagull shit—and flung it into his face.

He lurched back, wiping at his eyes with his free hand.

I scrambled over the side, swinging down the rungs.

Partway down, I glanced up and saw Dr. Matthews's furious face glowering over the side. "You won't get away this time!" he shouted. "I'll scrape you off like a leech!" Then he disappeared from my sight, obviously heading for his hover, to swoop down on me and knock me into the water.

My fast descent increased the strain on the rungs. I pulled one out entirely. It went spinning down to the water, and I barely managed to grab the next one to keep from falling after it.

I neared the bottom, my arms aching and my knees rubbed

raw. Out of the corner of my eye I saw a large, fast-moving shadow hurtling down—Dr. Matthews's hover—but it wasn't coming after me, it was plunging straight toward the water. It struck the surface with a heavy crash and began sinking in a cloud of bubbles. Startled, I lost my grip, kicked out the rung below me, and went sliding and clutching the rest of the way, flopping sideways into the water with an impact that jarred me from head to foot. Stunned, I managed to crawl up on the boat and untie it. I pushed off with one of the oars and began rowing.

When I got farther out, I could see the top of the Wall.

It was the patrol ursid—what I'd seen first as a brown speck—which had encountered the hover in its path and shoved it over the side.

Dr. Matthews hadn't been in the hover. He hadn't reached it.

He was still there, on top of the Wall.

And the ursid had grabbed him.

I could see the two figures together—the ursid reared upright on its haunches with its extensors clasping the struggling and helpless man. The signal light on the ursid's back was flashing—the hover call.

I kept rowing with slow mechanical strokes, dulled by the pain in my body and the terrific heat of the day. I could see that I had ripped out several of the lower rungs when I had gone crashing down. Climbing back up now—if I'd wanted to—would be impossible.

I rowed on. The Wall slowly diminished. So did the two tiny figures standing together on the top. The one on the right—Dr. Matthews—didn't seem to be struggling now.

I could still see the ursid's signal light flashing, but not until I had gone quite a distance across the flatlands, fighting the swells and the currents, did I realize that the call would go unanswered.

JULY 10

Twice a day I climb to the top of the maple to look out across the flatlands to the Wall. At this distance I can't see what I know is still there—what will remain there as long as the Wall stands—but I can see it in my mind's eye: the two figures, upright and immobile, locked together. Waiting.

It is horrible to think of it, but I suspect that by now the gulls will be gathering there.

JULY 11

From my observation post, I have noticed a change in the color of the water covering the flatlands. It is darker in places, heavy currents of brown and gray streaking the green of the sea.

Does this come from Rampart erosion or from within the Wall?

Sometimes I think I can hear the Wall—hear that deep, hollow bell-stroke booming—and I would say this was only my imagination, except whenever I have seemed to hear it, I have felt the wind in my face, blowing from that direction.

I have said nothing to Julia about the sounds I have heard or the dark currents I have seen, but she has sensed my anxiety and works beside me with fierce intensity from sunup to sunset.

We have finished the boat. We leave tomorrow. The logs are tight, the superstructure is in place. We have enough food and water for two weeks.

I have decided not to strike out across the Shelf from this point, but to work along the inland side of the Rampart, going south toward the Chesapeake Valley, where, as I remember, the water is calmer. We will make our open-water run to the mainland from there.

If there is time.

I have used the Librex to transmit the entire contents of the micropen—everything I've written—to a score of places: libraries, vidiprints, the Engineering Control Board, etc. Where this wounded and eccentric Librex has actually sent this material is another question, but at least I have the hope that what I have set down will survive me.

JULY 12

One year ago I began this record. It is an anniversary for me—
and for the Wall.

There probably won't be another one.

I climbed the maple for what may be my last look at it. It
seemed the same as when I first saw it many years ago—a solid
band of rock across the horizon and beyond my sight, beyond
my imagination, and yet I know it is broken in a dozen places,
and the entire Shelf is flooded, towns and roads and farms
drowned and coastal cities abandoned, the work of generations
lost forever. And the rest will fall soon. Nothing will be left except
the battered foundations deep in the sea and perhaps a few jagged
stretches rearing up here and there, populated by gulls and terns
and mollusks.

But the idea of the Wall will remain, at least for a time. A
memory. A whisper from the past. A reminder that there once
existed a community of humans capable of an undertaking requiring steady purpose, building for the future. For those yet to
come. Like the trees, casting seed.

The Wall was the last achievement of a society determined to
create something greater than itself.

When it was finished, something died—spirit, energy, faith.

The Wall is our tombstone.

She and I are like Adam and Eve, ignorant of life and of each
other, uninstructed. We must learn on our own, for we have
nothing behind us, no history, except for the Wall. When it
vanishes, there will be no past, and without past there is no future,
as without death there is no life.

We do not touch, but our eyes touch, our thoughts and feelings
touch. Today she smiled. I can hear the Wall and see the darkening
waters, yet we are linked by bonds of trust and confidence, she
has smiled, and the Wall still stands; there is hope.

But are we at the beginning or the end?

M